D1481748

The Condom Industry in the United States

The Condom Industry in the United States

by

James S. Murphy

McFarland & Company, Inc., Publishers
Jefferson, North Carolina, and London

British Library Cataloguing-in-Publication data are available

Library of Congress Cataloguing-in-Publication Data

Murphy, James S., 1934–
The condom industry in the United States /
by James S. Murphy.
p. cm.
Includes bibliographical references and index.
ISBN 0-89950-533-3 (lib. bdg. : 50# alk. paper) ∞
1. Condom industry—United States. I. Title.
HD9995.C63U66 1990
338.4'7681761—dc20 90-52637
CIP

Manufactured in the United States of America

McFarland & Company, Inc., Publishers
Box 611, Jefferson, North Carolina 28640

To my wife and children with love
And to Edward Nell with respect

Contents

8. Costs to Society

9. Industry Profits

10. Summary and Conclusions

List of Tables

List of Figures

Chapter 1
Introduction

Definitions

Webster's Dictionary defines a condom as "a thin protective sheath, generally of rubber, used to prevent venereal infection or as a contraceptive." This describes precisely the end products of the industry covered by this book. The term "condom" is also used by the medical profession to describe a part used to attach an external male catheter to a penis as part of an incontinence device. While this unit has the same physical structure and is usually made by the same companies, its market is small, its methods of sale and distribution are significantly different, and the product specification is considerably less rigorous. In short, broadening the scope to include this ancillary line would unnecessarily complicate my analysis.

Common usage has generated many other names for penis sheaths, including rubbers, prophylactics, safes, french safes, french letters, etc. However, none of these is as precise as condom, and they may not always have the same meaning to different individuals.

Condoms have been available for a long time. One firm, Schmid Laboratories, Inc., has been making them in the United States since 1888. Yet prior to 1986 condoms were a whispered, minuscule contributor to the economy. Birth-control devices have often been mentioned in off-color jokes and carried by adolescent males to demonstrate their virility, but they were seldom mentioned in polite society or in mixed company. Often they proved to be a source of embarassment to buyers, retailers, and even employees of the manufacturers.

In 1986 with the recognition that an epidemic of acquired immunodeficiency syndrome (AIDS) was in full swing, the surgeon general of the United States endorsed the use of condoms as the only currently available effective barrier against AIDS. The news media filled with discussions and reports on condoms. Manufacturers started advertising their products, and retailers moved their stocks from under the counter to highly visible positions in the store. A topic for blushing quickly became a cause célèbre. People became aware that condoms offered a chance that they and/or their children might avoid contracting a debilitating and usually fatal disease.

Need for This Study

The economic impact of the condom industry is far greater than its contribution to the gross national product or its traditional role in helping to prevent unwanted pregnancies would seem to indicate. Its greatest significance stems from the potential to help avoid some of the costs to society of AIDS and other sexually transmitted diseases (STDs). These diseases result in lost manpower, the diversion of resources, and considerable expense to provide health care for the afflicted. Estimates of these costs run into many billions of dollars. An industry which plays such a key role warrants study. Greater insight is needed concerning how this industry is structured and interacts with other industrial and commercial enterprises, as well as with governmental and educational segments of society. This knowledge could lead to further ideas about how to increase use of the only practical barrier protection available.

Studies of oligopoly predominantly focus on large-scale industries dominated by a few giant firms. In writing about oligopolies economists, such as Samuelson, Bain, Stigler, Sylos-Labini, et al., choose examples like steel, automobiles, textiles, oil, etc.—all very large industries. However, bigness is not a necessary criterion for this class of market structure. In order to identify an oligopoly we look for:

1. Few suppliers operating along cost curves where the efficient production level is large relative to the total market demand.

2. Comparative price rigidity with discipline maintained by some form of structural rigidity. Many oligopolists face a "kinked" demand curve around an administered price level. This occurs because price cuts are matched by competitors to defend their market share while price increases may not be followed.

3. Rivalry and competition which favors nonprice actions such as branding, advertising, displays, etc.

The U.S. condom industry meets these conditions, yet with only $246 million in sales in 1988 at market prices, it also ranks among the smaller segments of the economy. Therefore, an investigation into how and why this industry developed to its present form should be of interest to students of oligopoly.

An industry study describes the workings of a group of sellers of close-substitute products who supply a common set of buyers. Its purposes are to provide insight into how each segment in an industry works and relates to every other segment and the total economy. An industry study enables us to observe the organization and its behavior in relation to accepted economic theory. The objective is to determine how well the facts conform to theories that were abstractly formulated and generalized to cover a variety of situations. Unfortunately, the province of economics is so broad that any theory may not be applicable to all situations. No economist is all-seeing; he or she is seldom completely right or completely wrong. Therefore differences of opinion arise. This study of the U.S. condom industry provides examples relevant to a number of controversial economic theories and thereby helps improve our understanding of how they apply within one small segment of the economy. Included are:

1. The existence of the "kinked" demand curve. The validity of this concept has been challenged by a number of researchers (including Stigler, Simon, Primeaux and Bomball) and supported by other economists in addition to those originally credited with the idea, Paul Sweezy, R.L. Hall, and C.J. Hitch.

2. The process by which an administered, entry-restricting price is established. This was not dealt with adequately in the original presentations of the "kinked" demand curve.

3. The shapes of the short- and long-run cost curves which are relevant to the study of a modern firm or industry. The practical use of the concept of a long-run cost curve where all factor inputs are completely variable is questioned, and so is the use of a single short-run cost curve to describe behavior during both expansion and contraction.

4. The role of the government in defining the product, its costs, and method of sale for an item in commerce and the government's influence in the evolution of a particular organizational structure. The role of the government is more commonly viewed as breaking up oligopolies rather than fostering them and seldom is the control over all aspects of an individual consumer product discussed.

5. The existence of a strong oligopsony which limits an oligopoly's access to the consumer. This is a topic which has seldom been treated in the economic literature. Most writings on oligopsony and monopsony deal with the sale of raw materials to a manufacturer. The theories of oligopoly pricing rely on some form of structural rigidity to maintain discipline. The existence of an oligopsony that fulfills this function has not been shown before.

6. Nonprice competition other than advertising. Media advertising has limited value for condom manufacturers; therefore other types of nonprice competition are emphasized.

7. Welfare diseconomies that result from the nonuse of a product resulting in a substantial social cost. Most welfare economists have focused on the adverse effects of actions rather than the social costs arising from a lack of self-benefiting behavior.

Demand is a function of consumer acceptance. It is not simply the existence of a need identified by society or government. As protection against the transmission of sexually transmitted diseases, condoms fill an important societal need. However, the need exceeds the willingness of consumers to use these devices. There was a surge in the demand for condoms in 1986 and 1987. This triggered expansion by all condom producers. Unfortunately, consumer requirements did not continue to grow. This created two problems: manufacturers now have excess capacity, while the threat of STDs continues to increase because less than 25 percent of the sexually active population avails itself of the only practical preventive measure available. If demand is not substantially increased, manufacturers will lack incentives to improve their product and make it more appealing. Social costs will continue to escalate. This book discusses the means chosen to try to raise demand, and their successes and failures.

Methodology

This study follows the lines established by Professor Joe S. Bain, of the University of California, for industry studies. I will begin by outlining the structure of the industry, starting with a historical background and a description of the environment which caused the current competitive configuration and products to evolve. In order to complete the picture, some brief background information on other contraceptive devices and products will be reviewed.

Chapters 3, 4, and 5 provide detailed descriptions of manufacturing and sales within the condom industry. They deal with the following characteristics of the industry: concentration, economies of scale, points of entry, market share, methods of product differentiation, and barriers to entry. The industry is small and concentrated. Not all competitors start from basic raw materials (latex, etc.)—some purchase condoms in bulk which they then test, process, and package. Points of market entry also vary. This has led to the dominance of specialized markets by individual firms. The historical reasons for these positions and the currently emerging dynamics of the market are explored as well as the importance of the "countervailing power" (to use Galbraith's phrase) of the retailers.

The reason for the existence of any industry is consumer demand. Growth depends on increasing consumer usage and acceptance. For the condom business, these factors are intensified by governmental and societal needs to control the quality of the product and to promote its use. The current status of these stakeholders are explored in Chapters 6 and 7.

In Chapter 8 the economic impact of the failure to use condoms is investigated. Chapter 9 looks at company profits to seek some measure of the incentive for and the ability of the players to participate fully in successfully meeting the challenge ahead. The final chapter summarizes and concludes the findings of this study in terms of the standard parameters for an industry study and offers some personal observations.

Sources of Information

In the past the condom industry has been small and of inadequate significance to the overall economy to warrant serious investigation. As a result, little published information is available. Most of the recent data are in the form of journal, magazine, and newspaper articles. This book draws heavily on these sources as well as interviews with knowledgeable individuals in all facets of the industry. Since cost data on the condom industry are not published, it was necessary to utilize input from operating personnel within the industry to verify the reasonableness of the costs developed. Care was taken to avoid betraying any confidential information which could be attributed to a single firm or to individuals within a firm. The purpose here is to provide representative information, not to aid any competitive firms. All descriptions of trade and company practices were also checked by a number of former and current active participants in the industry.

Chapter 2

The Environment

Overview

Industries and the firms that comprise them evolve into a particular structure or configuration based on their history and a combination of societal, governmental, and competitive forces. Our understanding of the environment which created and sustains the condom industry starts with a history of the product, reviews the acceptance of birth control in the United States, and then charts the development of the condom industry. The picture of the competitive arena is completed by describing other contraceptive products and how they relate to condoms.

Historical Background

Physical penis coverings have been used for centuries to protect against pregnancy or infection, to decorate, and occasionally as a sexual stimulant during coitus. The use of sheaths can be traced back to 1350 B.C. when Egyptian men wore devices made of papyrus as phallic decorations and colored and undyed animal membranes in their more active sexual pursuits.

The first formal scientific presentation of the use of condoms as a preventive against disease came in the 16th century. The Italian anatomist Fallopius described the construction of linen sheaths in his work "on the preservation from French caries (syphilis)," Chapter 89 of *De Morbo Gallico* (1564). Protective devices fashioned from animal intestines soon followed. By the 17th century, condoms were being made from fish membranes and lamb intestines.

There is some dispute over how penis sheaths came to be called "condoms." Some say they were named after an English physician to King Charles II (1660–85) named Dr. John Conton (later corrupted to Con*dom*). Others ascribe it to an anonymous butcher who perfected the use of lambskin prophylactics and named them after his hometown, Condom, France. Another story is that it was derived from the Latin word *condus* which means one who collects or preserves something. The truth appears lost in history.

In the 18th century the use of the name *condom* came into vogue and the sheaths were popularized as a means of "protection from venereal disease and numerous bastard offspring." According to his memoirs, Casanova (1725–98) was among the first to popularize the use of condoms to prevent births. He apparently was also aware of the protection they provided against venereal diseases. Moreover, he seems to have tested the devices by inflating them with air.

Widespread use of condoms accelerated after the invention of vulcanized rubber in 1843–44. Condoms became far less expensive. During most of the 1800s and into the 20th century, the method of forming rubber condoms was by dipping wooden molds into a solution of rubber dissolved in naphtha and then curing the formed product. One writer stated that the glans condom was first introduced into Europe from America through the World Exposition held in Philadelphia in 1876. In spite of this technical breakthrough, rubber condoms remained inferior to those made from animal membranes until around 1920.

In the United States, federal, state, and local laws kept condom making and sale regional enterprises. The Comstock Laws of 1873 forbade any interstate commerce in contraception. In addition, the ability of manufacturers to collect lamb cecums was very limited. There is only one cecum, the preferred natural membrane, provided by each lamb slaughtered. Likewise, no organization existed to collect the materials from many abatoirs. With only a comparatively small number of cecums available from each slaughterhouse, the butchers had little incentive to organize their operations to save these parts of the offal. Thus, raw material supplies were limited, and condom manufacturers had to make local arrangements for their raw materials. As a result, less desirable membrane materials were used as well as small batches of natural rubber solutions. This localization contributed greatly to the slow development of more reliable contraceptive sheaths.

Birth Control

The effects of population growth has long been a subject for economists. Thomas Robert Malthus (1766–1834), the English economist, argued that population tends to increase faster than its means of subsistence. Therefore, unless population increases are checked by some means, widespread poverty and degradation would inevitably result. While Malthus urged moral restraint rather than contraception, birth control is a far more attractive alternative for limiting population than disease, famine, or war. Karl Marx (1818–83), the German economist, put great emphasis upon the reserve army of the unemployed, keeping wages at the subsistence level. The German Socialist leader, Rosa Luxemburg (1870–1919), while encouraging a birth strike in 1913, urged that working-class women should not "produce children who will become slaves to feed, fight, and toil for the enemy—Capitalism."[1] On a less extreme note, Margaret Sanger in 1920 drew on the wage fund theory when she wrote that "the basic principle of craft unionism is limitation of the number of workers in a given trade. . . . Every unionist knows, as a matter of course, that if the number is kept small enough, his organization can compel increases of wages, steady employment, and decent working conditions."[2] Birth control opponents retorted that smaller populations or populations growing less rapidly than in the past spelled decreased consumption, reduced production, and hence led to greater unemployment.

Surveys show that the appeal of birth control has had its greatest impact among the middle class. Birthrates have not fallen nearly so dramatically among the lower economic classes who should consider themselves the primary victims of the downward economic pressures of population increase. It has been the "selfish" middle class, striving to protect and improve its economic position, that has been most receptive to the idea of birth control. Family planning is more of an attitudinal problem than a technical or educational one. Lee Rainwater, after an extensive study, found that "very few couples of any class do not know of one or two methods they could use to control the size of their families. At the simplest level of knowledge, even the lower-class respondents seem at least as well equipped as were the highest status persons in Europe and England at the time these later groups began limiting their families."[3]

The appeal to the individual's self-interest in terms of protection against disease and the monetary burden of births has been the most attractive reason for the use of condoms. Governmental agencies and most religious organizations (some quietly and reluctantly) are influenced by the health aspects. Macroeconomic impacts may be of interest to scholars and society, but it is the very personal appeal to protection of an individual's physical and financial well-being that sells condoms.

Opposition to birth control on moral grounds has long been considered a key issue in preventing its wider practice. President Theodore Roosevelt held the belief that the family had a moral duty to serve the state: it should provide children to build national strength. He contended that Germany dominated Europe because she had "the welfare of the cradle . . . during the nineteenth century."[4] This statement seemed to express the general opinion of most Americans in the later part of the last century and into the early years of this one.

Religious organizations have long tried to keep people from sinning against God and nature through unnatural contraception. The debates on this issue have been well publicized and need not be repeated here. What is important is that the impact of these arguments, including the continuing very vocal objections of the Roman Catholic church and other orthodox faiths, seems to have had less success in terms of influencing behavior than the rhetoric indicates. Surveys conducted in 1936 by

Table 2A. Little Comstock Laws: Number of States with Regulations Restricting the Marketing of Contraceptives and Condoms as of March, 1973

Type of Legislation	*All Contraceptives*	*Condoms*
Prohibit Advertising	13	9
Prohibit Display	9	6
Require a License to Sell	5	9
Pharmacy Sale Only	9	8
Prohibit Vending Machine Sales	12	14

Note: These values are not additive. Data from 29 states were listed by the researchers who compiled the information used to prepare this table. Many states had laws restricting the marketing of contraceptives as a class and also specific statutes against condoms. Some states only restricted condom sales.

Source: This table is based on the work of Philip Harvey and Eve W. Paul as published in *The Condom: Increasing Utilization in the United States*, ed. M.H. Redford et al. San Francisco: San Francisco Press, 1974, 60.

Fortune magazine reported 63 percent of Americans, including 42 percent of Roman Catholics, believed "in the teaching and practice of birth control." By 1939, Henry Pringle reported in the *Ladies' Home Journal*, 79 percent of American women favored birth control. Four years later other polls indicated the figure had risen to 85 percent.[5] Thus, from a personal usage viewpoint, the impact of the moral judgments of various organizations appears to have had a declining influence on behavior. However, such organizations did exert a force on legislation which profoundly influenced the structure of the condom industry.

Most notable was the passage of the so-called Comstock Laws, a group of statutes passed in 1873[6] at the insistence of Anthony Comstock, leader of the Society for the Prevention of Vice. Their purpose was to protect sexual purity and, allegedly, suppress quack medical advertisers. The laws included sweeping prohibitions against mailing, interstate transporting, or importing "obscene, lewd, or lascivious" articles. While they did not define obscenity, they specifically banned all devices and information pertaining to "preventing conception."[7] In addition, 22 states had "little Comstock laws." As recently as 1973, many states retained laws restricting the sale, distribution, and promotion of condoms (Table 2A lists this information). The Comstock statutes did not forbid the manufacture or sale of contraceptives but did ban interstate commerce in these products. While evidence suggests that these laws were not always rigorously enforced, they undoubtedly fostered local enterprises. This led to a large number of small suppliers, limited value of trademark protection, and uneven quality standards.

Evolution of the U.S. Condom Industry

Julius Schmid, a former sausage skin-maker and founder of the present day Schmid Laboratories Inc., got his start in 1883 by acquiring a business that made bottle seals from animal membranes. These seals were used to prevent the evaporation of chemicals and high-priced perfumes. In 1888 Schmid began to use his experience with sausage casings and capping skins to manufacture prophylactic sheaths. Though he was not the first to manufacture such products in the United States, he pioneered the production of a standardized, safe, reliable condom of the highest quality. His products were never cheap and were often considered the best available. His guiding business philosophy was that consumers would pay more for a quality product to deal with life-affecting issues such as disease prevention and birth control. This concept proved equally valid for the Youngs Rubber Company, which later joined Schmid in dominating the U.S. condom industry.

Schmid formed condoms from the cecum of lambs. A cecum is the blind pouch in which the intestines begin and into which the ileum opens from one side. When detached and cleaned, the cecum forms a natural condom sheath. There is only one cecum per lamb. (Other animals have cecums, but the lamb's is the proper size and shape for a condom.) The units must be washed, defatted, fitted with a mechanism (e.g., a spring) to hold the condom on the penis, and carefully packaged to prevent damage. The collection of cecums and the amount of hand labor required to transform them into condoms has always made the skin condom substantially more expensive than rubber units.

Up until the 1920s most condoms, especially those made of rubber, were of questionable quality. Rubber condoms were hand dipped from rubber cement. In 1919 Frederick Killian started hand dipping condoms from natural rubber latex at his plant in Akron, Ohio, using a process developed by the Goodyear Rubber Company. In 1921 Fred's brother Burkhardt joined the firm and developed a patented process for continously dipping condoms from latex. In 1924 Merrill Youngs, President of the Youngs Rubber Company, began purchasing condoms in bulk from Killian and packaging them for resale. In 1934, responding to government pressure, because they had a monopoly on the technology, Killian leased a condom manufacturing line and the accompanying technology to Youngs Rubber.[8]

Also around 1920 Julius Schmid purchased a plant in Germany to continually make condoms by dipping forms into a naphtha solution of natural rubber. The plant was dismantled and reassembled at Little Falls, New Jersey. This process was more easily controlled than ones based on latex. Schmid used this "cement dipping" method until 1963, when he converted to latex because of fire hazards experienced with the cement process. Neither the EPA nor OSHA would likely permit such a process today.

Merrill Youngs was an astute marketer. He recognized very early that the government and most members of society found the disease prevention and other health aspect of condoms to be their most acceptable feature. Condoms would be better tolerated as health preservation aids than as contraceptives. The natural outlet for their sale was the pharmacy. Therefore, at a time when other manufacturers would sell to any retailer (barbershops were a popular outlet), Youngs sold his "Trojans" exclusively to druggists. His success formula was simple: provide a high-quality, reliable, branded product that could not be purchased through any other type of outlet. The price was kept high to assure the pharmacist the highest unit profit of any item in his store. This provided a tangible incentive to promote Youngs' Trojan brand and formed the foundation for Trojans becoming synonomous with condoms for many Americans.[9]

In the early years, trademarks for condoms were seldom honored. Manufacturers stole the popular names used by others. ("Merry Widows" was one of the most popular during these times.) Under the Comstock acts, interstate commerce in condoms was illegal; thus it was considered unlikely that anyone could sue and win trademark protection for an illegal venture. In 1927 C.I. Lee and Company of Chicago, Illinois, noticed that Trojans were very popular, high priced, and sold only through drugstores. Lee proceeded to copy the Trojan name and to package and sell the product to whoever would buy it. This incensed Merrill Youngs and he sued. The United States district court initially dismissed the case. On appeal, however, Judge Thomas Swan of the United States Court of Appeals for the Second Circuit effectively qualified the language of the Comstock Laws for purposes of trademark enforcement. He distinguished between legitimate and illegitimate use and held that the statute only prevents the latter. "The intention to prevent a proper medical use of drugs or other articles merely because they are capable of illegal uses is not lightly to be ascribed to Congress."[10] He wrote that the sale of condoms through drug outlets was a legal use. The United States Court of Appeals for the Second Circuit virtually nullified the Comstock Laws with regard to contraceptives. The judge ruled that condoms were capable of a legitimate use, subject only to the test of intended purpose. The prevention of conception, where that is not forbidden by local law, was a proper medical purpose.

The soundness of Judge Swan's reasoning was cited in several subsequent cases and culminated in a sweeping decision by Judge Augustus Hand. Judge Hand said that the Comstock Laws should not be taken literally. He noted that in 1873 information on the possible dangers of conception was very meager. The law should be construed as including "only such articles as Congress would have denounced as immoral if it had understood all the conditions under which they were to be used. Its design, in our opinion, was not to prevent the importation, sale, or carriage by mail of things which might intelligently be employed by conscientious and competent physicians for the purpose of saving life or promoting the well being of their patients."[11] The legal debate did not end here; but for most purposes this decision made birth control legal. Swan's findings put teeth into the enforcement of trademark rights for condoms. Merrill Youngs further sought to strengthen his brand by actively promoting the passage of state and local laws requiring the licensing of purveyors of condoms. This boosted the position of the druggist, Youngs's relationships with them, and the popularity of the Trojan brand.

While there is no documented evidence, it seems reasonable to assume that then, as now, competitors closely monitored each other's strategies and adopted the best. Youngs followed the Schmid philosophy of selling standardized, reliable merchandise at a premium price. Schmid joined in the efforts to make pharmacies the exclusive purveyors of condoms. While Youngs focused on building its business on the East Coast, Julius Schmid sent his son Carl to the West Coast and Canada, locations where Schmid's Ramses and Sheik brands became preeminent. In 1949 Schmid's market share in the West approached 90 percent and in Canada surpassed 95 percent.

In the period starting in the mid–1930s Youngs Rubber Company and Schmid Laboratories, Inc., consolidated their holds on the market so that in recent years together they accounted for about 84 percent of the U.S. retail market for condoms.

Other Contraceptives

Technically, condoms should only be compared with other contraceptives sold over the counter. However, the birth control pill has had such an impact on the condom market that it cannot be ignored in this study. The pill, a prescription product, captures the largest number of retail dollars for birth control products. In 1974, when use of the pill was at its peak, over ten million American women were taking it. Since then this market has dropped to around six million as a result of adverse publicity. Women remain skeptical about the pill even though the formulations which led to serious complications and unpleasant side effects are no longer on the market. It is claimed that three out of four women cling to the notion that the pill creates considerable health risks.[12] More recently, a 1987 survey conducted for the Ortho Pharmaceutical Corporation shows "a reversal of the decline among married women between 1973 and 1982."[13] There are over sixty brands of birth control pills on the market, differing more in promotional schemes than in composition.

The attractions of the pill over condoms include:

1. No artificial barriers between sex partners to interfere with sensitivity.

2. No interruption of the romance of the moment.

Table 2B. Contraceptive Choices: Percentage of U.S. women aged 18–44, fertile, sexually active, and not pregnant or seeking pregnancy, who said they were using a specific contraceptive or contraceptives

Method	*Total*	*Married*	*Unmarried*
All	93%	97%	87%
Sterilization	36%	51%	13%
–Female	22%	28%	12%
–Male	16%	24%	1%
Pill	32%	22%	48%
Condom	16%	15%	16%
IUD	3%	3%	3%
Diaphragm	4%	4%	4%
Foam	1%	3%	1%
Cream/Jelly	*	*	*
Suppository	1%	1%	1%
Sponge	3%	1%	4%
Per. Abstinence	5%	5%	3%
Withdrawal	5%	5%	6%
Douche	1%	1%	1%
No Method	7%	3%	13%

* *Less than 0.5%*

Source: J.D. Forrest and R.R. Fordyce, "U.S. Women's Contraceptive Attitudes and Practice: How They've Changed in the 1980s," *Family Planning Perspectives* 20, no. 3 (May/June 1988). Copyright The Allen Guttmacher Institute.

---

3. The female is in complete control; she need not seek the cooperation of her partner.

4. Privacy—no one need know she is using a contraceptive.

5. No need to carry devices.

These attractions led to a significant decline in the demand for condoms during the period from June 1960, when the Food and Drug Administration sanctioned the use of synthetic oral anovulants for contraception[14] till 1974. While condom sales increased after 1973, this growth was not as dramatic as the decline of use of the pill.

Table 2B lists the contraceptive choices of sexually active women in the U.S. between the ages of 18 and 44 in 1987. This table is based on a survey for the Ortho Pharmaceutical Corporation by Market Facts, a professional marketing research firm. From these data the dominant roles of the pill and condoms become apparent.

An IUD, an intrauterine device, is a mechanical appliance placed in the female's uterine cavity to prevent the implantation or growth of an embryo. Like the pill, IUDs provide no protection against STDs. However, they were a very popular contraceptive measure up to the mid-1970s. The reasons for this popularity were similar to those for the pill. In 1971 pelvic infections started to be traced to the use of some IUDs, especially the Dalkon Shield manufactured by A.H. Robins, Inc. By 1974 it was believed that some IUDs cause an increase in pelvic inflammatory disease (PID), an ascending infection of the uterus, ovaries, and fallopian tubes. As a result of this belief and subsequent liability concerns, IUDs now have only a minor role in contraception.

Contraceptive foams, creams, jellies, and suppositories are forms of vaginal spermicides, agents that destroy spermatozoa. They are inserted in the vagina. Because they are safe and uncomplicated, spermicides have long been used to protect against pregnancy. Spermicides are detergents that kill in vitro a number of organisms responsible for sexually transmissible infections, including gonorrhea, trichonomas, herpes, chlamydia, and AIDS viruses. To be effective these products must be placed deep inside the vagina near the cervix and used consistently. Foams, creams, and jellies are most often used in conjunction with barriers such as condoms or diaphragms. Nonoxonol-9 is currently the most widely used spermicide.

Vaginal suppositories attracted considerable attention when introduced in the mid–1970s. Irritation problems were encountered with some of the early products. At present contraceptive suppositories hold only 1 percent of the market.

The FDA approved the first vaginal contraceptive sponge in 1983. The product is a small pillow-shaped polyurethane sponge that contains 1 gram of nonoxonol-9 spermacide. It has a concave dimple intended to fit over the cervix and decrease the chance of dislodgement during intercourse. Its advantages include ease of use, lack of the potential side effects associated with the pill, and the ability to remain in place for 24 hours. The sponge offers some protection against STDs, but it is not as effective as a condom in preventing either contraception or STDs. The sponge has captured a niche position among devices used by women in spite of some claims that the sponge's use can lead to toxic shock syndrome.

Table 2C lists the retail dollar sales of contraceptives in the U.S. in 1988. The pill, with a better than 80 percent share, dominates. Condoms, the leading OTC (over-the-counter) contraceptives, are a distant second with just under 16 percent. Taken together all the other products make up around 4 percent of this business.

Insights

The insights yielded by the investigations covered in this chapter include:

Table 2C. U.S. Contraceptive Market, 1988

Product Category	*Estimated Sales ($ million)*	*Percent*
Pill	$1,250	80.3%
Condoms	246	15.8%
Jelly	20	1.3%
Sponge	12	0.8%
Diaphragms	10	0.7%
Suppositories	8	0.5%
Foams	8	0.5%
Creams	2	0.1%
Total	$1,556	100.0%

These estimates were calculated based on personal study, published company reports, and insights provided by knowledgeable persons in the industry.

First, legal restraints caused by the Comstock Laws kept the condom industry localized until the first quarter of this century. As a result, condom manufacturing was kept small and fragmented. There was insufficient demand in each geographic market to foster innovation in manufacturing techniques. Consequently, economies of scale were impractical. Since markets could not be expanded, the incentive to improve the product, thereby delivering greater value to the consumer, was uneven and local.

Restrictions against advertising and the dissemination of product information led in many instances to the consumer receiving unsatisfactory products. Confusion was further strengthened by the clandestine nature of condom sales through establishments (barbershops, saloons, etc.) with no purpose other than profitably catering to the prurient interests of their customers. The product and the industry were generally considered disreputable. By keeping the condom industry fragmented, the government thwarted two functions of an economic system: the efficient allocation of resources and the capability to improve and grow. The reason for this hindrance was the government's moral judgment that birth control was sinful.

Second, the growth of Youngs Rubber and Schmid Laboratories was based on their recognition of the consumer's desire for a standardized, reliable condom and the pharmacy's role as the natural outlet for contraceptive sales. These factors combined to develop a strategy based on products that commanded a high price and yielded one of the most profitable products sold by druggists. Local laws restricting the sale of condoms to pharmacies gave the druggist a monopoly. By catering to the pharmacist, Youngs and Schmid developed an oligopolistic position in supplying condoms. Laws forbidding the advertising or open display of contraceptive products made it difficult for new firms to enter this business.

Third, Youngs' vigorous defense of the Trojan trademark led to the legalization of condoms in interstate commerce for all practical purposes. This action worked to expand the market for condoms and prevented the copying of trademarks which established a means of product differentiation. Thus, the Youngs and Schmid merchandise became better known with each sale and gradually built another barrier to new entrants. Prior to the *Youngs* v. *C.I. Lee* case there was no value to condom brand names or trademarks. With legal enforcement of brands, customers now had a means of distinguishing among products. Product differentiation coupled with the potential for national sales through interstate commerce created an incentive for greater efficiency of manufacturing and standardization of products.

Fourth, knowledge of the use of condoms is widespread. Appeals based on the need to restrict population growth, morality, or general health appear to have little effect on the use or nonuse of condoms. Only entreaties to the selfish self-interests of the individual work. As Thomas Malthus wrote in *An Essay on the Principal of Population*, "The effects on man are complicated. Impelled to the increase of his species by an equally powerful instinct, reason interrupts his career, and asks whether he may not bring beings into the world, for whom he cannot provide the means of support. . . . The preventive check peculiar to man, arises from his reasoning faculties, which enable him to calculate distant consequences." It is only by appealing to this reasoning and making the appeal very personal that new users will be induced to buy and use condoms regularly, thereby expanding the market by catering to fundamental consumer needs.

Chapter 3

The Manufacturing Structure

Overview

Commercially available condoms fall into two categories based on the raw material used: lamb cecums or natural rubber latex. As discussed earlier, condoms have been made from lamb cecums for centuries, and continue to have a following in the United States. They account for around 20 percent of the retail dollars spent on condoms and about 5.5 percent of the volume; these percentages indicate the high unit price of lamb cecums relative to the latex product. With minor exceptions, primarily in terms of automated handling equipment, the manufacturing process is relatively unchanged since Julius Schmid started using lamb cecums a century ago. The biggest advance has been in collecting the cecums. New Zealand, the lamb capital of the world, is now the prime source and initial processing center. Schmid Laboratories and Carter-Wallace (the current owner of Youngs Rubber) are the only producers of these products. After further cleaning, defatting, and salting, the raw skins are shipped to finishing plants. Schmid's facility is in Puerto Rico and Carter-Wallace's in Trenton, New Jersey.

The market niche for the skins is small and not growing. Only cecum collection meets the oligopoly requirement of a large production level relative to the market. Smaller volume units than those operated by Schmid and Carter-Wallace probably would not offer sufficient incentive for the abatoirs to separate, handle, and collect the skins. The rest of the processing uses mostly manual labor and offers little in terms of economies of scale. Therefore, no further consideration will be given to natural skin condoms in this study.

There are five companies manufacturing condoms from natural rubber latex in the United States. This chapter describes the production process. It is essentially the same for all participants. The purpose is to provide an understanding of how the method of making these products may contribute to the industry's oligopolistic structure. The firms will be described relative to their manufacturing capabilities. Understanding them involves not only the domestic operations but the international connections which could effect their relative manufacturing prowess as well. The concentration of production capabilities will be covered apropos the unique traits of each firm.

Table 3A. Flow Diagram of Condom Manufacturing

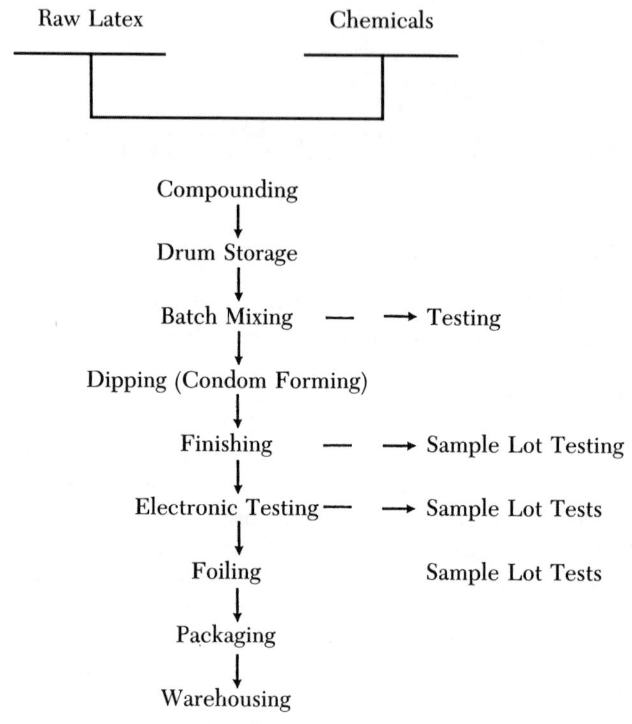

Costs will be presented showing the effects of economies of scale and investigating the strength of such economies in terms of barriers to entry. Finally, international sourcing will be discussed. The United States has comparatively open markets for foreign goods. With the spotlight on condoms fostered by the AIDS epidemic, it is only natural that this once sleepy market should attract competition from off-shore producers.

The Manufacturing Process

Table 3A shows the flow of the latex condom production process. It starts with delivery of the raw natural rubber latex and other raw materials. The ingredients are carefully tested. Natural rubber latex, as its name implies, is a naturally occurring material. Therefore, it is subject to substantial variations resulting from climate, soil conditions, etc. As a result, it is not as consistently uniform as synthetically produced materials. Latex is an emulsion or dispersion of tiny rubber particles in water. It is not a solution. Consequently, care must be taken in selecting other ingredients which will attach to the rubber particles during compounding. These ingredients, while small in quantity, are necessary to vulcanize the rubber and aid in processing. "Vulcanization" is the term used to describe the chemical linking of the rubber particles that makes the final product strong, durable, and fit for commercial use. By varying the ingredients used and their quantities, it is possible to adjust the physical properties of the product. "Fast" or "hot" curing systems often yield high tensile strength, shorter elongation, and, generally, a more limited shelf life.

Condoms require good stretch properties, moderate burst strength, and good aging characteristics. Consequently, the condom-forming process usually uses a "slow" cure system based on sulfur. The raw chemicals are generally premixed to form a paste and then blended with the latex in the compounding operation. The compound is unloaded into drums for storage. Typically, compounded latex is allowed to remain in drum storage for seven or eight days before it is ready for use in the dipping operation. The reasons are to effect a precure—i.e. to let the vulcanization process start to work—and also to allow any air which was trapped during compounding to exit the material (air bubbles cause flaws in condoms). The compound is tested by simulating forming before it is added to the condom dipping machine. While the dipping process is a continuous operation, compounding is done in batches. Therefore, it is essential to be certain that the latex compound already in the system is not contaminated with a "bad" batch.

The dipping machine is a long, hooded machine about one-third the length of a football field (i.e., 100 ft.). Thick tempered glass rods move along a closed belt between two circular gears, similar to the fan belt of a car. The belt drags the rods, called "mandrels," through a series of dips into the latex compound. The mandrels rotate to spread the latex evenly. Between dips each coat is hot air dried (i.e., partially cured). Several coats are used to build the condom to the required thickness. After the final dipping and drying, the condoms are automatically rolled off the mandrels.

The next step is to finish the condom by coating it with talc or other powder material to prevent the rubber from sticking to itself. This takes place in a tumbling machine (usually a washing machine without an agitator).

After a postcure period of several days, the condoms are sampled by lot and tested. One test involves filling the condom with air until it bursts. (Condoms usually stretch beyond the required 1.5 cubic feet, about the size of a watermelon, before bursting.) Another test requires filling a condom with 300 ml. of water and inspecting for pin holes.[1] Batches passing these representative destructive test samplings then undergo electronic testing. Every condom is tested for pin holes. In this stage each condom is mounted on a stainless steel mandrel which passes into a water bath. An electric charge is passed through the water. If any holes are present, a circuit will be established with the steel mandrel and the condom will be rejected. If the condom is pin hole–free, the rubber will prevent a circuit from being completed.

Condoms which pass this test are automatically rolled and proceed to the packaging lines to be individually wrapped in plastic film (called "foil" because metal foil was long used for this purpose). If the condom is to be lubricated, with or without spermicide, the lubricant is applied dropwise by a metering pump just prior to adding the top wrap in the foiling operation. After the process is completed, the condoms are once again sampled by lot and destructively tested.

Condom dipping machines are designed to run continuously, preferably 24 hours a day, 7 days a week. Under ideal conditions cleanup and preventive maintenance are conducted every tenth day. Firms with several lines shut down one and keep the others running. A cleanup takes 8 to 10 hours. Therefore, it is costly to shut down frequently. Partially cured compound can not be left in the dip tank to contaminate future production. Machinery needs to be cleaned and oiled. Corrosion is an ever-present danger with water-based processes. The electrical and mechanical equipment must be well maintained. Any interruption of production is costly. Even when demand is low, the machines are run continuously, with four or five days between cleanups. At such times the shut-down periods are extended to limit output.

Identification of the Firms

Five firms produce condoms from latex in the United States; other firms that claim to manufacture condoms usually start with untested condoms purchased in bulk. Two of these five, Carter-Wallace and Schmid Laboratories, dominate the retail market. Ansell Inc. provides most of the condoms purchased by the U.S. Agency for International Development (U.S.A.I.D.), the largest buyer of condoms in the word—U.S.A.I.D. supplies condoms to underdeveloped nations in order to promote birth control. Safetex Inc., until recently Circle Rubber, has been a minor participant in the retail market and a supplier of bulk condoms to other firms. Killian Latex produces condoms on a contract basis for Carter-Wallace.

Ansell Inc. manufactures dipped latex products—gloves, balloons, and condoms—in countries around the world as part of Pacific Dunlop Ltd. Pacific Dunlop is an Australian firm which reported $US 3.3 billion in sales in 1987. About 40 percent, or $130 million, of Ansell's $336 million in sales in 1987 was generated in North America. Ansell is a manufacturing and technology–driven company. Their basic growth strategy has been to acquire firms with good positions in a market or product line and then take whatever steps are necessary to become the low-cost producer.[2] Most of

Ansell's condoms are produced in the United States at plants in Dothan and Troy, Alabama. Ansell has a base load of three million gross of condoms a year which are manufactured for the U.S. government (U.S.A.I.D.). Ansell's total productive capacity is estimated at around four million gross a year. Ansell is also a major supplier of household, industrial, and medical examination gloves made in their plants in Malaysia and Thailand.

Carter-Wallace is an established supplier of consumer and health care products with sales of $483 million worldwide and $372 million in the U.S. for the year ending March 31, 1988.[3] Carter-Wallace purchased the Youngs Rubber Company in 1985 and thereby entered the condom business. Their condom capacity is estimated at around 1.5 million gross a year.

Schmid Laboratories is the condom producer most clearly dedicated to contraception. Their other product lines include diaphragms, contraceptive jellies and creams, douches, etc. Schmid is owned by the London International Group (LIG) with sales of $445 million for the year ending March 31, 1988.[4]

LIG is the largest manufacturer of condoms in the United Kingdom with the dominant market share. This company also has condom plants in Germany, Italy, and Spain plus an arrangement (undoubtedly technical and probably including part ownership) with a firm in India. LIG is a major producer of rubber gloves in Malaysia. Its latex products worldwide are probably on a par with Ansell Inc. However, while Ansell is technically driven, LIG's primary focus has been marketing. Schmid's condom plant in Little Falls, New Jersey, has around 1.2 million gross a year capacity.

Circle Rubber U.S.A., Inc., was started by the Fuji Latex Co. in 1975. The Circle plant in Newark, New Jersey, had half a million gross a year capacity before it was shut down during the summer of 1988. Prior to final closure of this plant, the FDA required them to discontinue production for a time in order to correct lapses in their manufacturing practices. Circle produced sheaths for companies who start with purchased bulk condoms.

The parent, Fuji Latex Co., is the second largest condom manufacturer in Japan. They have a 32 percent Japanese market share behind Okamoto's 50 percent share. Seventy percent of Fuji's three million gross a year production in Japan is exported to Europe. Recently Fuji built a plant in Chester, Virginia, to replace the troubled Circle facility. This plant is a joint venture with Nisho Iwai America Corp. and operates under the name Safetex Corporation. Annual production capacity has been reported at one million gross.[5]

Killian Latex Co. is a small, family-owned and operated latex compounding operation in Akron, Ohio. During the condom boom of 1987 Killian rebuilt a condom machine that had been dismantled as part of a contract agreement when Ansell acquired the Akwell operation in 1975. This unit is capable of producing around 700,000 gross of condoms a year.

Killian, coming full circle, is once again making condoms for the Youngs Rubber division of Carter-Wallace. Killian's business, including both condom and latex compounds, has always focused on manufacturing for marketing astute firms. Their technical capabilities are well respected with regard to latex compounding and processing.

Manufacturers have roughly comparable in terms of manufacturing efficiency. The dipping, testing, and packaging facilities are similar. Total U.S. demand for condoms during 1988 is estimated to be around six million gross, about equally split between the retail market and the U.S.A.I.D. purchases. This compares to the roughly 8.5 million gross of dipping capacity calculated above.

However, when the opportunistic production of Killian, the new excess capacity of Safetex, and the traditionally idle line at Ansell are subtracted, the total capacity of the traditional marketers totals around 6.5 million gross. Comparing this to the six million market figure illustrates how the tight supply situation occurred in the retail market in 1987, when the FDA recalled considerable quantities of finished condoms. (Another factor, overbuying by retailers, will be discussed later in this book.)

Concentration and Unique Positions

Manufacturers have unique characteristics from which they draw operational strengths. Carter-Wallace's Trojan trademark is the strongest in the country. They continue to enjoy about 56 percent of the retail market, assuring them a strong production base.

Schmid Laboratories, as part of the London International Group, can draw on technology from worldwide condom manufacturing units. In addition, their historical position in the U.S. market provides a strong cadre of customer loyalty. Schmid currently has a 26 percent share in branded latex condoms.

Ansell, with its sales to the U.S.A.I.D. program, operates the largest condom manufacturing facility in the country. Coupled with a strong technical orientation, it is reasonable to assume that they are the low-cost producer. In addition, during 1987 they were able to gain some retail market share based on their ability to supply from usually idle capacity.

Safetex has a new plant based on Fuji's extensive production experience in Japan. If Safetex can generate sufficient sales to utilize most of the capacity of this plant, it is unlikely they will be at any cost disadvantage.

Killian is a small entrepreneurial firm able to act quickly on the opportunities of the moment. Considering the fact that they rebuilt an old dipping line, it is doubtful that they have invested heavily in this business. Their break-even production volume is likely much less than that of the other players due to low overheads.

Cost Factors

The investment required to enter the condom business is not large in an absolute sense. Safetex reported that it spent $10 million in 1988 to build a new plant in Virginia capable of making one million gross of condoms a year; this represents a unit investment cost of 7 cents per condom, a comparatively small sum in today's capital market. Thus, it is reasonable to conclude that capital requirements provide little barrier to entering this business.

As pointed out earlier, a condom dipping machine must be operated continuously. While some downtime can be scheduled, there is a finite limit to its use. Inactivity causes rapid deterioration of the equipment. (Maintaining a plant on standby is much different than the complete mothballing which preserved the equipment that Killian rebuilt. The equipment is like a watch; if it doesn't run, the mechanisms clog and rust.) The key to operating the machinery is to sell products. The total market is small relative to the capacity of a dipping machine. Consequently, a producer must capture a large share of the demand in order to operate efficiently.

Manufacturing costs are confidential. No firm will reveal its costs because of the competitive advantages such information would give competitors and customers. In order to illustrate the effects of volume on costs, I have calculated estimates. The values and assumptions used are shown on Tables 3C, 3D, and 3E and graphically depicted on Figures 3.1, 3.2, and 3.3. These are not the actual costs of any firm. They were calculated based on public data and suggestions from knowledgeable individuals. The resulting numbers were subsequently checked for reasonableness by other persons active in the industry. They are representative but may be lower than financial accounting values used by firms. Corporations often include other factors, which are important to them, but not considered relevant within the scope of this study. The costs presented here are adequate to demonstrate the effect of volume and the relative importance of manufacturing costs to the industry.

Cost curves are important tools of microeconomic analysis. They are used to help understand and explain the relationships among the level of output, the social and private costs of production, and—when combined with revenue curves—profits. Most presentations of cost curves deal with abstract concepts and lack the specificity possible with an example taken from actual operations. Because the condom industry is relatively uncomplicated, it provides an opportunity to explore the meaning and use of cost curves more closely.

Common usage is to combine all costs in developing the average cost curves. Greater insights are possible if the manufacturing costs are considered separately before becoming part of the combined operating costs. (This follows the Marxian concept that all surplus, or profit, is generated by production and realized through the sale of the product.) This section of the condom study deals with manufacturing; in Chapter 9 production costs become part of the total cost and revenue analysis.

Manufacturing costs, including raw materials, labor, capital consumption allowances, and manufacturing overheads, are a necessary portion of the operating costs but do not represent a complete picture. The cost of producing condoms as a percentage of total costs varies with output. At lower levels of output, when the fixed costs are spread over fewer units, the ratio of manufacturing costs to total costs (which also include selling, general and administrative expenses, plus a minimum return on capital) is lower. In the production range of 500,000 to 1,000,000 gross of condoms a year, the manufacturing costs in my example vary from 34 to 41 percent of the total costs. Manufacturing costs are usually a smaller share (compared to condoms) of total costs for most health and beauty aid products. Costs associated with selling, administration, and finance, including interest charges and minimum returns on capital employed, add significantly to the total cost. Therefore, judgments made on the basis of the methods of manufacture alone may not sufficiently describe the workings of an industry's cost structure. Likewise, combining costs prematurely could inhibit understanding the interplay of forces within an industry.

By separating the analysis of manufacturing costs, it is possible to test some assumptions by economists who pioneered the study of imperfect competition. For example, both Joan Robinson and E.H. Chamberlain assumed that the demand and cost curves for individual producers are alike. This fits the manufacturing structure of the condom industry. The technical requirements of forming condoms are fixed scientifically. (There are few variations possible in formulating thin-walled vulcanized natural rubber latex products and any options which may exist are unlikely to measurably change the manufacturing costs.) Produce specifications and quality assurance requirements are set by government regulation (this topic is covered more fully in Chapter 6). Because of the small relative sizes of the industry and the condom plants, manufacturers have little influence over the costs of labor or materials; they simply pay the going rates. Variable costs do not appreciably change with shifts in output. The assumption of constant marginal cost is not only based on observed condom industry behavior, but is also supported by empirical studies cited by Sylos-Labini in his book *Oligopoly and Technical Progress.*[6] Sylos-Labini found constant marginal costs to be characteristic of conditions for most manufacturing firms. Joel Dean is another economist who found marginal costs to be constant.[7] Any manufacturing cost differences, other than those that are volume-related, are a function of the geographic location of the plants. However, as will be discussed in later chapters, there are differences in selling, administrative, and capital costs which to some extent explain variations in profits among firms. These nonmanufacturing charges reflect the "diversity of conditions surrounding each producer" referred to by Chamberlain.

Several conditions were postulated in order to make the cost analysis in this study as realistic as possible. Major condom producers operate more than one production line. This provides a measure of safety in case of breakdown and permits staggered maintenance without a complete shutdown. Most plants are capable of making more product than is indicated by their rated capacity via faster line speeds, more intensive operation, etc. For this book the rated capacity was taken as the lowest cost production rate. Beyond this point the average cost curves were extended in an upward arc to reflect that greater output is possible at increasingly higher variable costs caused by overtime, a higher rate of rejects, more frequent or extensive maintenance, etc.

As noted from the data (see Tables 3D and 3E and Figures 3.1, 3.2 and 3.3) condom manufacturing is volume-sensitive. Average costs fall rapidly before reaching the optimum level.[8] The reason is obvious: most costs are fixed. Consequently, the larger the volume, the lower the average cost. Adding another line in an existing plant boosts costs in the short run but not as sharply as would be the case with building a new facility. The additional fixed charges are incremental. The result is that less extra demand is needed to regain and drop below the previously attained minimum average manufacturing cost. In my example it is about half.

The above analysis assumes that the facility is built large enough to accommodate two lines and the second line is only purchased, installed, and staffed when justified by demand. If the entire plant were built at once, this would increase fixed expenses, raise average costs in the lower output range, and produce a smooth continuous average cost curve with the same low cost at the one million gross level as illustrated by Figure 3.3. The effect of treating this operation as a single entity is that average costs are higher over a wider span of output.

Both curves are representative of typical experience. Firms add capacity as their business grows (see Figure 3.1.). Once capacity is added, if output falls costs retreat along the curve shown on Figure 3.3—higher average costs—because the firm has added the equipment and infrastructure to support a higher level of output. (Most firms operate more than two lines at a plant site. However, the average costs do not differ appreciably and the simplified presentation used here is more easily explained while remaining a reasonable representation of reality.)

U.S. retail sales in 1988 totaled three million gross of condoms. Therefore, the volume of production needed to operate efficiently (above 500,000 gross on the graph) is large relative to this market.

Cost Curves

The use of "U"–shaped average cost curves is a standard convention in economics. This configuration serves to demonstrate that costs typically fall as production increases, reflecting the ability to allocate fixed costs over greater quantities of output and to lower variable costs or at least hold them constant. However, a point (the low point on the "U"-curve) is eventually reached where the fixed portion of the average cost is so low that the impact of additional output is negligible.

There are few instances where once this lowest cost level of output is reached no further production is possible. Generally, most equipment can be operated more intensively than its rated capacity. Beyond the lowest cost production level variable costs start to rise. Some examples as to why this may occur include overtime pay for workers, higher reject rates due to operating the equipment at faster line speeds, more frequent breakdowns, mistakes made as operators attempt to conform to a more rapid pace, etc. The graphs used in this study are drawn with dotted lines beyond the low point to reflect that while greater output is known to be feasible, the precise effect on costs has not been documented. When the point of greatest efficiency is approached, most firms tend to add equipment—as shown in my example. Few professional managers are willing to conclude that they have reached their peak efficiency and therefore will not expand operations. The most common assumption is that past growth will continue and a new lower cost level can be attained by adding more equipment. Higher average costs are tolerated while capacity is being expanded. This is considered a temporary cost of growth.

The downward sloping (improving) segment of the manufacturing cost curves are relatively accurate in terms of describing how costs change while output is expanding. However, the increase of average costs in response to declining demand (i.e., moving back up the curve to the left) is not quite so clear. When production is being curtailed, inefficiencies not present during expansion are encountered. For example, it may not be possible to lay off labor as quickly as production drops, worker's attitudes may change as they see their jobs threatened, the utilization of raw materials could increase as operators become less efficient, etc. Production curtailment is an area that managers would rather not consider and as a result seldom study in advance. Most executives prefer to cope with such a situation only if and when it develops. The most likely scenario is that during a contraction period costs will generally retreat along a line parallel to and higher than the original cost line.

Likewise the combined costs shown on Figure 3.3 are more apt to be representative in the downward, expansion direction rather than a leftward contraction. Inefficiencies such as those cited earlier force the curve to shift toward the upper right-hand corner.

Figure 3.3 can also be considered illustrative of the industry average cost curve. If the costs of each producer are similar, then only the values along the horizontal axis need be changed in order to represent the industry (e.g., the output quantities multipled by 2 for two producers, 3 for three, etc.).

Cost-curve analysis is a subject which in recent years has not attracted a lot of attention from economic writers. A search of the *Economic Literature Index* revealed only 19 articles on this subject published between 1969 and 1988. Of these only one was as recent as 1987 (Revier) and the majority of the theoretical papers were published in 1976 or earlier. For the most part, economists seem comfortable with the current state of the theory on this subject. However, occasionally articles are written on the long-run cost curve, betraying some unease with this aspect of the topic. A sampling of articles illustrates these misgivings. Sylos-Labini wrote, "if the series of smaller plants corresponding to different technologies is not continuous—that is, if there is no general transition from one plant to the next—then we cannot properly speak of a curve even on this (decreasing) side of the limit (minimum cost) represented by the biggest plant. In these conditions there is, in strict analysis, no such thing as a long-run supply curve."[9] Another well-known economist, Jacob Viner, first contended and later retracted the idea that the long-run average cost curve "is drawn so as to connect the points of lowest average cost for each scale of plant,"[10] a condition which proved mathematically impossible. Chang, writing in the *Quarterly Review of Economics and Business,* considered this to be simply "a matter of mathematics."[11] Chang claimed that "there seem to be absurdities involved in adapting the theoretical analysis to a chart such as this (the LAC curve)." Chang continued by postulating that the problem could be solved by showing the short-run curves with "V" shapes, so that the minimum costs for each short-run condition would lie along the LAC. He based his argument on "the fact that in the real world, even with given technical conditions, the divisibility of plant can hardly be infinite; and therefore the actual LAC curve should be a real curve consisting of the least cost-points of the SAC curves . . . this is in no way intended to modify the conditions of the short-run average cost . . . but to make legitimate the relationship between the long-run and short-run average cost curves." Professor A. Ross Shepherd refuted Chang's argument by showing that the minimum SAC points can indeed stand off the LAC, but these points would represent costs which are higher than could be attained by switching to the next higher size plant whose curve is tangent to the LAC but not necessarily at the minimum of the SAC.[12] (If the LAC is not tangent at the low points, is it a valid depiction of technical progress?) Other studies by Giora Hanoch[13] and Charles Revier[14] showed that mathematically the expansion path (the LAC) can be concave as well as convex to the production line even though the short-run curves are always convex. This research illustrates the underlying discomfort that some economists have with the traditional concept of the long-run cost curve as an envelope of the SACs. Each of these papers provided insights into specialized situations. However, they do not help with understanding the modern manufacturing growth situation where capital is added in step increments and fixed costs are a significant portion of total manufacturing costs.

Many writers (e.g., Beattie and Taylor,[15] Rowe,[16] Kelly and Waldman[17]) seem more concerned with the mathematical derivation of a curve enveloping the SACs than whether it is a realistic presentation of the actual state of events. Somehow the fact that cost curves are visual aids for understanding plant operations has been confused with a drive for mathematical precision. (Other references to more published articles on cost curves are listed in footnotes 18, 19, and 20.)

I contend that the problem with most studies of the LAC curve is that the authors are trying to force-fit a historical pattern onto a diagram intended for cost analysis. When more than one SAC curve is drawn on a single chart, it is intended to show that different plants or plant additions can produce different quantities of goods at different costs. Time is not one of the coordinates. There is no rule which says a line enveloping independently derived curves provides a reasonable representation of progress over time. Nor can a LAC drawn in this way be interpreted in the same manner as a SAC.

It seems more sensible to use the standard production line based on isoquants and input factors to illustrate long-term changes in output because in such charts an array of factor combinations are shown for each level of output. For the analysis of quantity changes on manufacturing costs in modern practice where the interrelations of factor inputs are fixed, SAC curves are the preferred diagrams. Capital and/or technology additions trigger the need for new average cost curves.

Each new plant or output segment carries its own set of fixed and variable costs. These costs must be added to any existing costs and a new curve which depicts the firm's or industry's revised operations developed. If the new output facilities are added to existing facilities in order to cover the entire range of output, then a new curve must be drawn which incorporates the fixed and variable costs of all units. If the "new" replaces the "old," the former SAC curve no longer exists and the new curve should cover the entire range of output. If the intent is to produce an industry cost curve (i.e., the old and new plants may represent competitors which exist at the same time), then a curve which incorporates the costs of both must be constructed. Only in this way is it possible to analyze the way manufacturing costs change relative to volume. Being two-dimensional, a graph can be used to show changes of only two variables at a time. It is unreasonable to expect a graph to accurately depict the relationship between costs, volume, and time simultaneously. Likewise it is misleading to incorporate two curves which must be interpreted differently in the same diagram.

The above refinements do not negate the use of cost curves but rather emphasize their importance in terms of showing and understanding the movement of costs in response to shifts in demand. They also demonstrate the value of studying manufacturing costs separately from the other components of operating costs in comprehending an industry.

Table 3B. Relative Costs in Condom Manufacturing

Cost Item	*% of Total*
Raw Materials	
Latex	6.3
Other Materials	1.3
Subtotal Raw Materials	7.6
Direct Labor	6.3
Overhead	15.9
Bulk Condom Cost	29.8
Testing	
Labor	8.9
Overhead	24.4
Subtotal Testing	33.5
Packaging	
Materials	15.7
Labor	5.2
Overhead	15.7
Subtotal Packaging	36.6
Total	100.0

These relative costs were developed based on personal knowledge of the industry plus input from informed industry sources and tested for reasonableness by individuals responsible for various aspects of condom manufacturing costs as well as data available through the Freedom of Information Act. They do not represent the accounting costs of any one firm.

Factor Inputs

Condom producers are not large users of labor and materials. Generally, marginal costs can be assumed to be constant (i.e., set largely by the technology and government regulation). Thus the spread of fixed costs over increasing volumes of output is the greatest determinant of falling average costs. However, manufacturing skill is an obstacle to entry by new firms into the condom industry. Latex is a naturally occurring product, subject to all the variations that nature can provide. These variations often cause temporary but significant shifts in factor inputs and costs. Therefore, the production of condoms requires as much of the art of experience as science. Certainly the requisite skills can be acquired through hiring experienced personnel, etc. However, as demonstrated by recent product recalls, even knowledgeable operators have trouble from time to time. The manufacture of condoms uses a combination of equipment and skilled people. Gaining knowledge to operate a specific facility takes time. While a large company can certainly afford the investment, any realistic analyst must question whether such a small market is worth the effort to a new entrant. Because

Table 3C. Nominal Natural Latex Prices for the U.S. East Coast

Year	*$ per Dry Pound*
1973	0.39
1974	0.58
1975	0.39
1976	0.50
1977	0.55
1978	0.63
1979	0.74
1980	0.95
1981	0.70
1982	0.63
1983	0.70
1984	0.71
1985	0.64
1986	0.65
1987	0.72
1988	1.09

All values are nominal prices. They are not actual prices which are negotiated separately by each firm on a contract basis. They are median values between the high and low prices quoted in the middle of each quarter during the year.

Source: The Goodyear Rubber Plantation Company.

---

material costs represent only 7.6 percent of condom manufacturing costs, as shown on Table 3B, wide fluctuations in the costs of specific ingredients, as illustrated by the nominal latex prices for the period 1973–88 shown on Table 3C, have little impact on the cost of a condom.

International Sourcing

During the 1987 surge in condom demand, strains were placed on available capacity by a combination of strong demand and unprecedented recalls due to an accelerated inspection program by the FDA. In an effort to fill customer orders, several firms purchased foreign-made condoms. The U.S. firms helped these off-shore producers gain FDA approval to sell their wares in the United States. Additionally, packages had to be imprinted with the country of origin. Foreign manufacturers thereby became acquainted with the opportunities in the U.S. market, their products were approved, and American consumers learned that condoms from overseas are of acceptable quality. The true impact of these actions may not be felt for several years, but the U.S. producers may have invited significant competitors to their party.

Table 3D. Assumptions Used in Estimating Manufacturing Costs for Condoms Made and Packaged for Retail Sale

A.) The reported Safetex capital cost of $10 million for a plant capable of producing one million gross of condoms a year was used.

B.) Each condom dipping line has a rated capacity of 500,000 gross of condoms a year, based on 7 day a week operation, 24 hours a day, 300 days a year.

C.) The $10 million investment is 50% equipment and 50% facilities.

D.) 5.5 cents a condom is a reasonable manufacturing and packaging cost at full rated capacity of 1 million gross of condoms a year.

E.) *Variable Costs*

raw materials (condoms & packaging)	$1.85/gross
labor (mfg., testing, & packaging)	$1.62/gross
variable cost/gross to rated capacity	$3.47/gross

F.) *Fixed expenses, first line*

capital consumption allowances	
*building (25 yr. depreciation)	$ 200,000
*equipment (10 yr. depreciation)	$ 250,000
overhead expense (66%* of full output)	$2,500,000
total fixed expense, one line	$2,950,000

G.) *Fixed expenses, second line*

capital consumption allowances	
*equipment (10 yr. depreciation)	$ 250,000
overhead expense (34%* of full output)	$1,275,000
total fixed expense, 2nd line	$1,525,000

* These percentages were arrived at using the "six-tenths" factor, a technique often used by engineers to roughly estimate costs associated with new capital investments. According to this technique when output is doubled, fixed charges often rise to 1.5 times (i.e., $2^{0.6}$) the original value.

Source: These assumptions started from a knowledge of actual costs which were then generalized and modified to produce reasonable representations of industry costs but not reflect the actual experience of any firm. The values were reviewed by a number of individuals in a position to know condom manufacturing costs and the interrelations of the input factors. The significance rests with the relationships of the numbers, not in the stated values.

As shown on the chart of relative cost factors (Table 3B), labor and overhead are significant cost elements. If demand can be captured, low-wage areas such as Malaysia and Thailand, where the latex is grown, are natural places to manufacture condoms.

Quality

Because of strict governmental enforcement of quality standards, there is little differentiation of condoms possible on this basis. All condoms sold

Table 3E. Output Data for Cost Curves

Output (M gross/yr.)			*Total Cost ($Mil./yr.)*			*Avg. Cost ($/gr.)*		
Line 1	*Line 2*	*Combin.*	*Line 1*	*Line 2*	*Combin.*	*Line 1*	*Line 2*	*Comb.*
100	– –	100	3,292	– –	3,292	32.92	– –	32.92
200	– –	200	3,634	– –	3,634	18.17	– –	18.17
300	– –	300	3,976	– –	3,976	13.25	– –	13.25
400	– –	400	4,318	– –	4,318	10.80	– –	10.80
500	– –	500	4,660	– –	4,660	9.32	– –	9.32
500	100	600	4,660	1,867	6,527		18.67	10.87
500	200	700	4,660	2,209	6,869		11.05	9.81
500	300	800	4,660	2,551	7,211		8.50	9.01
500	400	900	4,660	2,893	7,553		7.23	8.39
500	500	1,000	4,660	3,235	7,895		6.47	7.90

in the U.S. must comply with A.S.T.M. Specification D 3492–83. No lot of condoms may be sold if, on sampling, more than four condoms in one thousand fail to pass. Consequently, quality is not a property on which firms compete.

While the rejected product does not reach the market, the quality level during manufacturing impacts costs. Testing represents 33.5 percent of manufacturing costs. In addition, the higher the reject rate, the higher the average cost of the saleable product. The level of operations influences rejects. Typically, with continuous processes, up-to-rated capacity, workers and machines build a rhythm which improves efficiency. Interruptions to this flow, such as more frequent or longer shutdowns, lead to increased product loss. Output is usually lower and the percentage of rejects higher until the equipment is operating in its normal range. Workers also lose their edge with stoppages. Thus, as output drops, costs rise more than proportionately.

Insights

In analyzing the manufacturing sector of the condom industry in terms of the characteristics of an oligopoly and barriers to entry, the following insights became apparent:

First, standard condom dipping equipment has a high level of output relative to the market size. Thus, a manufacturer must capture a significant portion of the total market in order to compete profitably. The fixed expenses for manufacturing condoms are high relative to the total manufacturing cost. As output increases, these fixed charges are spread over larger quantities and decline on a unit basis. Figures 3.1 and 3.3 show that the average cost of a condom drops quickly as production rises. Beyond a certain point (around 500,000 gross in the example) the effect of this distribution of fixed expenses becomes less dramatic.

Each of the curves in Figure 3.1 represents a short-run situation (time periods during which certain inputs, in this example fixed manufacturing equipment, cannot be changed). The curve in the lower range of output (the one on the left) depicts a single manufacturing line capable of producing up to 500,000 gross of condoms a year. If the business grows, another production line can be added (the curve on the right) which takes advantage of some existing expenses and shows the effects of economies of scale.

Figure 3.3 illustrates the combined effect of these actions i.e., the long-run cost curve for a condom manufacturer. Typically, economic textbooks define the long run as "a period of time of such length that all inputs are variable." They then proceed to show a long-run cost curve as an envelope encompassing a series of short-run cost curves. This presentation is confusing and not particularly useful in analyzing a manufacturer's operations. In the short run, the factors of production are indeed fixed over a given range of output. However, investments made to increase output also fix the factors of production at the time they are put into operation. Seldom is the old unit scrapped when a new unit is added. If a new productive unit replaces a prior one, then an entirely new cost curve must be drawn covering the complete production range—not just the section where the new increment was added. Short-run cost curves are only integral parts of the long-range cost curve when both units operate to make up a firm's or an industry's total capacity. The only variability is in the choice of the increments of investment. These need not be technical duplicates of the first line as assumed in my example. They may be more efficient or use a different combination of factor inputs. But in order to be part of the long-run cost curve, they must only account for part of the total production. This describes a frequent occurrence whereby a manufacturer adds new facilities as the demand for his products justifies. Such additions generally take advantage of the latest technology and economies available from combination with existing operations. Once an incremental expansion is completed, the resultant cost curve becomes fixed and includes the costs of each short-run curve. The result is a series of new average costs for every level of output (i.e., a new average cost curve of the type illustrated by Figure 3.3). The slope of this curve is based on combining all the fixed costs to determine the intercept at zero output and then spreading the total over increasing numbers of units of production.

Second, the required investment, at $10 million to produce one million gross of condoms a year, is large enough to discourage easy entry by small entrepreneurs. By itself, the money required is not sufficient to deter a well-financed entrant. However, the combination of capital investment and technical skill requirements forms a more effective barrier to new entrants than either impediment could provide singly.

Figure 3.1 Average Costs of Condom Manufacturing

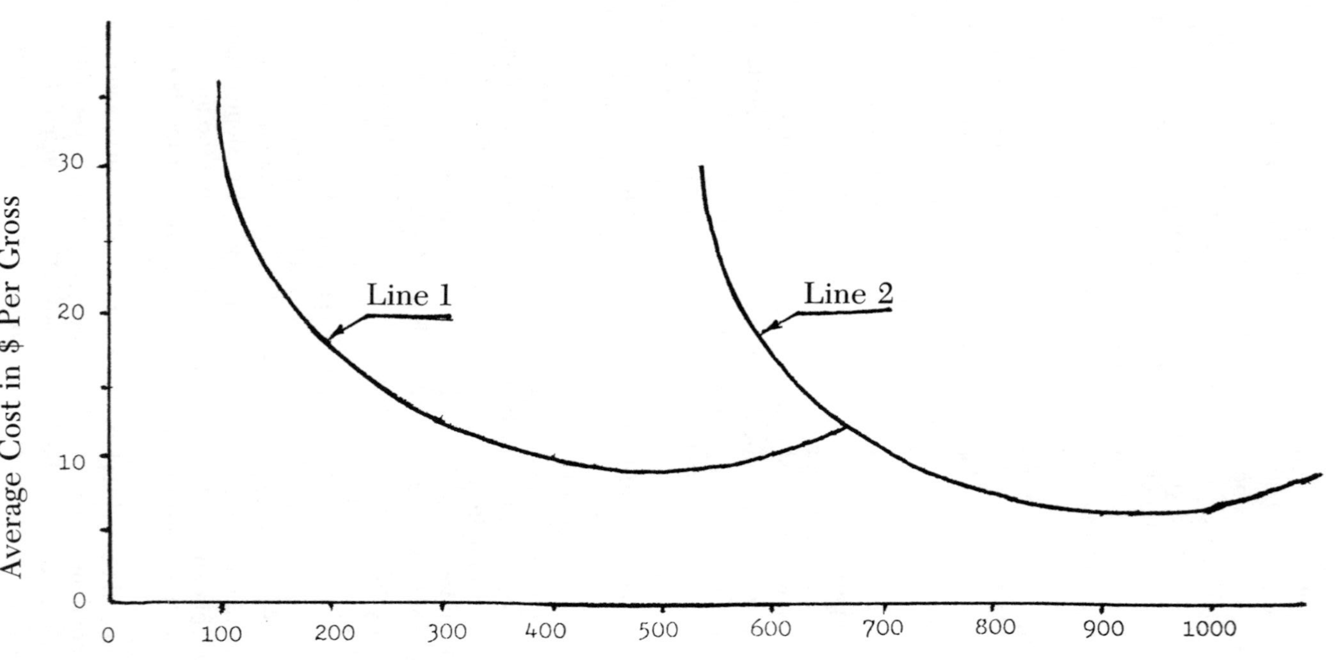

Figure 3.2 Total Costs of Condom Manufacturing

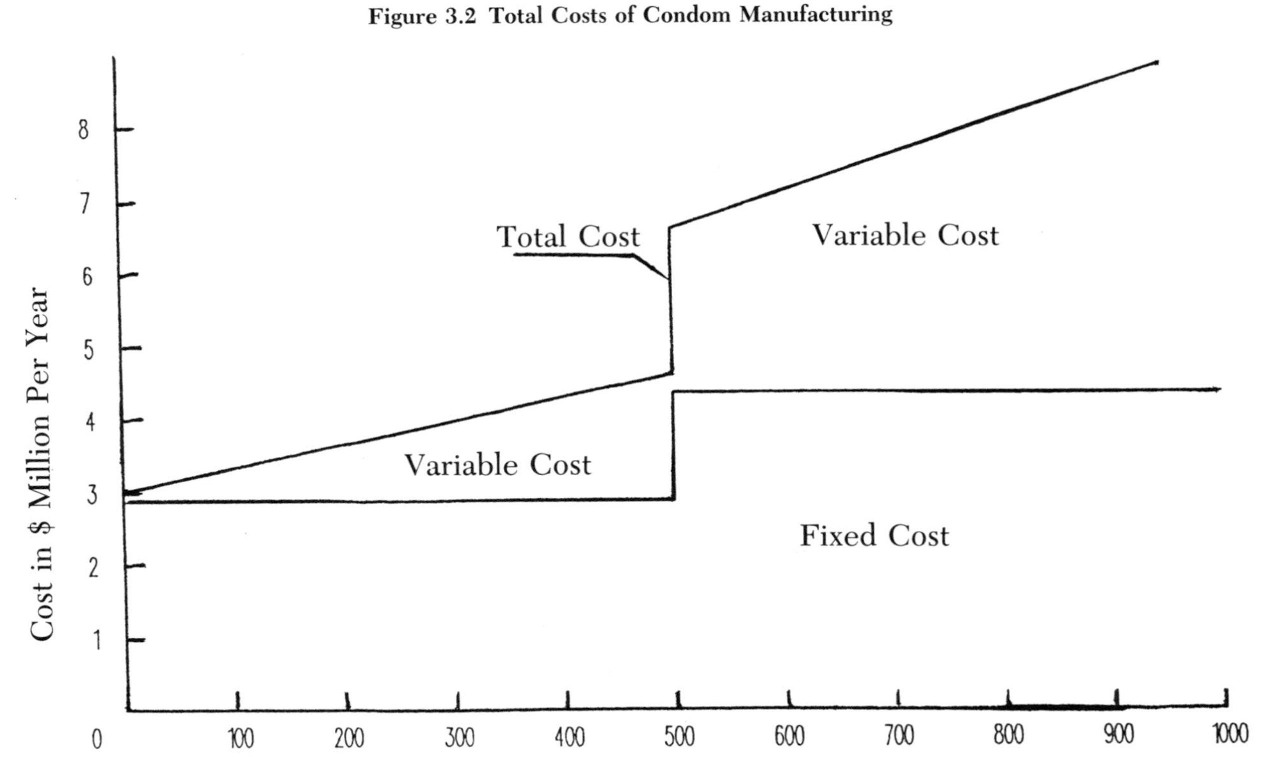

Figure 3.3 Average Costs of Condom Manufacturing Single Line

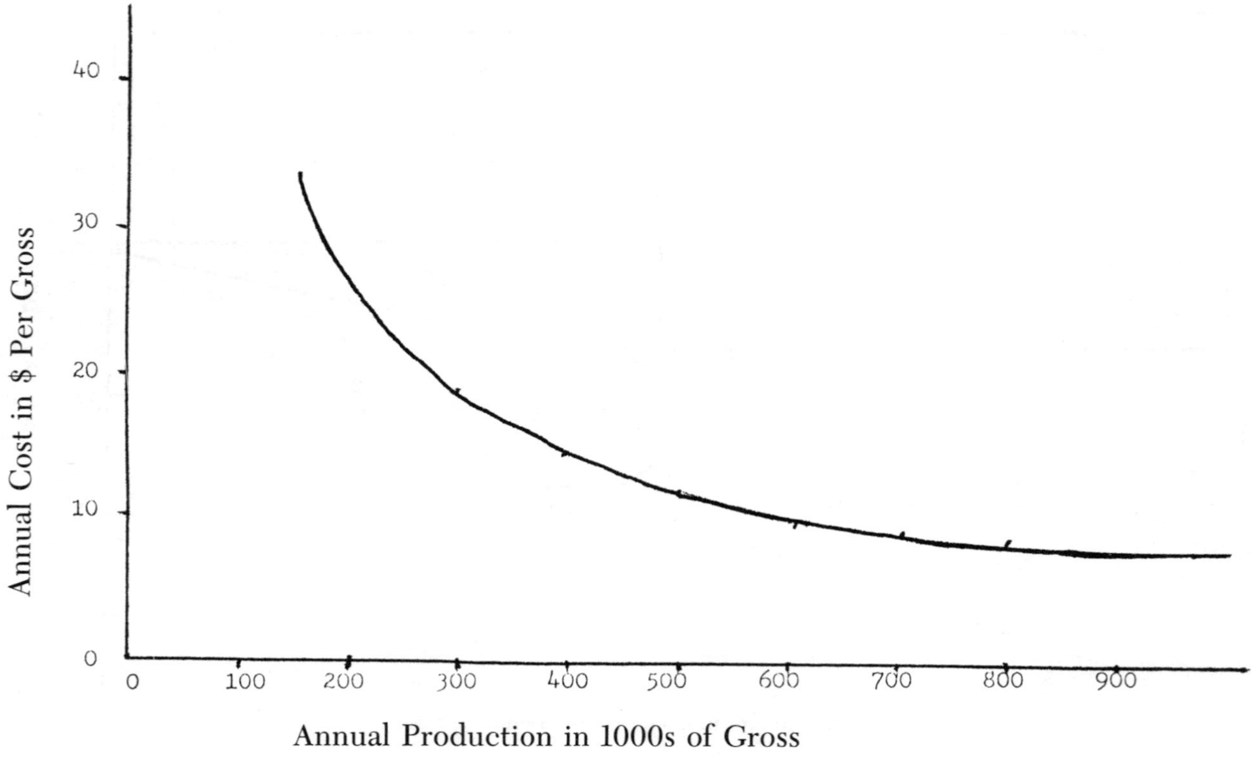

Third, high operating rates are necessary for the efficient utilization of the factors of production in condom dipping. Because of the need to operate the equipment continuously, unit raw material and labor costs rise more than proportionately when shutdowns are frequent or lengthy. At operating values lower than the rated capacity of the machinery, the cost curves slope upward sharply. Because of inefficiencies that enter into the production process during periods when the output is being curtailed, the actual unit costs are apt to be higher than experienced during expansion (i.e., it is more costly to retrench than to expand).

At throughputs beyond 500,000 gross a year, the savings available from more effective incremental use of the factors of production decline significantly. This is because the fixed costs are already allocated over such a large quantity of condoms that the effect of each additional unit on average cost becomes smaller and smaller; and the opportunities for savings in variable costs diminish as the labor and machines approach their level of peak efficiency. Therefore, beyond a certain point fine tuning of plant operations yields diminishing returns on the time, cost, and effort invested. While operation beyond the most efficient output level is known to be possible, the path of the average cost is not accurately defineable. This is a range of output which is considered temporary, and the added costs are an acceptable cost of expansion.

One of the concerns frequently voiced about oligopolies is that, in terms of welfare, they may use more units of resources than is necessary (i.e., they do not operate at their minimum cost). This may be true in an absolute sense, but the manufacturing cost of condoms is so low relative to the consumer price that the impact of any such inefficiencies is likely to be slight. The amount of each factor of production used in a small business such as condoms is barely measurable in terms of the allocation of society's resources.

Fourth, the smallness of the total condom market is a major factor in discouraging new condom manufacturers. Demand for condoms is not growing rapidly. Therefore, a new entrant would have to take market share away from established manufacturers in order to operate efficiently along a reasonable cost curve for this industry. (There is not sufficient information available to develop an industry cost curve showing each competitor's costs from the most to the least efficient. However, with little differences in technology, it seems reasonable to assume the cost curves will all be very similar.) It would not be practical for a new domestic manufacturer to slowly build a market position. Ansell, with the strongest manufacturing base in the U.S., as the main supplier of condoms to the U.S.A.I.D. program, has not been able to make sizeable inroads into the retail condom market.

Importers are not subject to this restraint since their manufacturing efficiencies are based on worldwide, not solely U.S., market penetration.

Chapter 4

The Distribution Structure

Overview

The channels through which products reach the consumer are important to all manufacturers. They are particularly crucial to the U.S. condom industry. With a comparatively small market and a continuous production process capable of producing large quantities of condoms, it is essential to capture a major share. It was by focusing on an exclusive market—pharmacies—that Youngs (now Carter-Wallace) and Schmid achieved dominant positions in this business. As long as drugstores were the exclusive legal purveyors of condoms and remained small entities, it was virtually impossible for other manufacturers to break into the U.S. retail condom market. Others had to concentrate on less profitable outlets such as government agencies (Ansell) or vending machines (National Sanitary Laboratories). In recent years the situation has changed. Nondrugstores which had long shunned condoms because of possible negative consumer reaction, loss through pilferage, slow turnover, etc., now sell them. Retailers have grown and consolidated to a point where large, professionally managed firms now dominate.

In addition to the five firms that manufacture condoms from latex, there are a number of companies which start by purchasing condoms in bulk. The amount of processing done by these organizations varies. Mentor Corporation, for example, tests the condoms, adds an adhesive for securing the condom to the penis, and a sleeve for applying the condom. Mentor then adds a lubricant and packages their unique product. National Sanitary Laboratories (NSL) tests and packages products for machine vending and some over-the-counter outlets. Numerous other firms merely package condoms, mostly for sale through vending machines. All of these firms are small. Mentor Corporation with $40 million in sales, primarily of surgically implanted prostheses, reported under $2 million in condom sales for the year ending March 31, 1988.[1] National Sanitary Laboratories, Inc., had total sales of around $7.7 million, of which about $5 million is estimated to be condom sales.[2] Between $2.5 and $3 million are accounted for by the machine vending segment.[3] The remaining participants are significantly smaller. The importance of these players to this study is in relation to their

Table 4A. 1988 Retail Market for Condoms in the U.S.

Outlet	*$ Million*	*% Share*
Drugstores	$157	64.0%
Food Stores	37	15.0%
Mass Merchants	25	10.0%
Machine Vending	25	10.0%
Mail Order	2	1.0%
Totals	$246	100.0%

These values were calculated based on several reports and personal surveys of the machine vending and mail-order distribution channels.

---

product innovation (Mentor) and their ability to capture a major share of a particular market niche (NSL).

Pharmacies no longer enjoy a monopoly on the sale of condoms. Mass merchandisers and food outlets have been obtaining a rising portion of this market. In addition, the drugstore itself has changed significantly. Gone are many of the "mom and pop" operations. Chains now dominate, and independent druggists have turned to cooperatives and large wholesalers to remain price competitive. Chains accounted for 73 percent of the condoms sold through drugstores in 1988.[4] There has also been increased use of vending machines to sell condoms. The idea is to make condoms ubiquitous (i.e., always readily available to potential users).

This chapter explores the main condom outlets, how they contributed to the oligopolistic position of the major brands, and to what extent changes in the structure of these distribution channels may impact the future structure of the condom industry.

Pharmacies

As mentioned earlier, pharmacies played a pivotal role in the development of the market position of the major brands. In courting pharmacists and promoting them as the exclusive legal outlet for condoms, Youngs and Schmid were able to build their brands and achieve preeminent positions in the consumer market. Drugstores remain the largest outlet for condoms, accounting for almost two-thirds of retail sales. (Table 4A lists the major retail outlets for condoms and their 1988 sales and market shares.)

In the 1920s, when branded condoms started to expand nationally and high-volume automated condom production was introduced, most pharmacies were independent, single-store operations. Chain drugstores, formerly only a small part of this business, started to blossom. The growth

Table 4B. Ten-Year Drugstore Sales Trends ($ Billions)

Year	*Total Indus.*	*% Chg.*	*Total Chain*	*% Chg.*	*Total Indep.*	*% Chg.*
1986	$50.2	7	$30.2	7	$20.0	7
1985	47.0	9	26.2	11	18.8	6
1984	43.2	9	25.5	12	17.7	5
1983	39.7	10	22.6	11	16.9	8
1982	36.2	8	20.5	11	15.7	5
1981	33.4	10	18.5	12	14.9	8
1980	30.3	12	16.4	16	13.9	7
1979	27.2	12	14.2	17	13.0	6
1978	24.3	10	12.1	16	12.2	4
1977	22.2	8	10.4	14	11.7	4

Note: Chain sales are for companies with four or more stores.

Table 4C. Evolving Character of the Chain Drug Industry

	No. of Companies		*%*	*No. of Stores*		*%*
Chain size	*1976*	*1986*	*Change*	*1976*	*1986*	*Chg.*
2–3 Stores	2,154	1,093	–49%	4,859	2,518	–48%
4–10 Stores	491	337	–31	2,599	1,901	–27
11 or More	173	120	–31	11,399	17,511	+54
Total Cos. with 2 or More Stores	2,818	1,550	–45	18,857	21,930	+16

Source: Tables 4B and 4C were reprinted by permission from *Drug Store News,* 13 April, 1987. Copyright Lebhar-Friedman, Inc., 425 Park Avenue, New York, N.Y. 10022.

---

of chains paralleled the rising popularity of preformulated drugs and medicinal preparations that were sold over the counter. Soda fountains became popular additions to stores, and product lines expanded beyond the traditional medicines. As pharmacies gradually changed into purveyors of increasingly diverse consumer goods and services, a trend toward agglomeration occurred. Stores merged into small chains. Chain drug companies bought other chains, continually increasing the concentration within this distribution channel.

During the 1950s self-service merchandising, which appears to have started during the worker shortages of World War II, came of age, and the concentration of the industry further accelerated. By 1986 chains represented 37 percent of the drugstores in the United States, up from 29

Table 4D. Ten-Year Drugstore Growth Trend

Year	*Total Stores*	*Chain Stores*	*Chain Share*	*Indep. Stores*	*Indep. Share*
1986	52,800	19,412	37%	33,388	63%
1985	52,500	18,550	35	33,950	65
1984	52,139	17,677	34	34,462	66
1983	50,264	16,733	33	33,531	67
1982	49,400	16,347	33	33,053	67
1981	49,310	14,864	30	34,646	70
1980	49,192	14,815	30	34,377	70
1979	48,822	15,110	31	33,712	69
1978	49,151	14,709	30	34,442	70
1977	49,397	14,530	29	34,867	71

Table 4E. Mass Merchandisers with Pharmacies in 1986

Company	*Total Stores*	*No. of Stores with Rx Depts.*	*% of Total with Rx Depts.*
K-Mart	2,066	1,022	49
Wal-Mart	1,009	474	47
Fred Meyer	94	88	94
Venture	167	96	57
Pamida	166	30	18
Target	252	18	7
Fedco	9	9	100
Cook United	30	8	26
Ames	321	9	9
Gold Circle	76	7	9

Source: Tables 4D and 4E were reprinted by permission from *Drug Store News*, 13 April, 1987. Copyright Lebhar-Friedman, Inc., 425 Park Avenue, New York, N.Y. 10022.

percent in 1977, a 34 percent increase in ten years. As measured by sales dollars the growth was even more dramatic. In 1986 chains accounted for 60 percent ($30.2 billion) of all retail pharmacy purchases compared with 47 percent in 1977.[5] Table 4B charts the year-by-year changes in sales of chain and independent drugstores from 1977 to 1986. Table 4C demonstrates the accelerated trend toward larger chains. The number of companies within each size category shrank while the number of stores operated by chains with 11 or more units expanded rapidly. The total number of stores operated by chains grew by one-third, and the number of independents drifted slowly downward. (This is illustrated by the values on Table 4D.) The largest 50 American drug chains represented 93 percent of chain sales (56.3 percent of all drugstore sales) in 1986. Each of the four largest chains operated over 1,000 stores and together accounted for 33.5 percent of the chain drugstores and 12.3 percent of all drugstores.[6]

In recent years chain drugstores have branched even further afield by adding deep discount units and wider varieties of merchandise. As reported in the *1988 Annual Report of the Chain Drug Industry:* "Deep discounting—once considered just a fad—is now firmly entrenched in today's retailing environment. There are an estimated 400 of these retailing powerhouses in operation, capturing between 3 and 4% of the total drugstore volume . . . procuring merchandise is a precarious situation for a deep discount store. It is a tricky balance and one that requires buying to hover around 80% on deal."[7] ("Deal" refers to discounted prices from producers. At various times during the year, manufacturers have sales similar to retail outlets. "Deal" is the term used for these sales. If products are always on deal, the list price becomes meaningless.) The quoted statement illustrates the pressure on chains to drive the price as low as possible.

As a result, purchasing has moved from the pharmacist/proprietor to a professional buyer. Computer-aided ordering and inventory systems control transactions. With this transition, past personal loyalties have eroded. No longer do drugstore purchasing agents view Youngs (Carter-Wallace) and Schmid as "White Knights" who helped them capture a lucrative product niche. Today's buyers probably were not born when this occurred and have no personal stake in the historical relationship. Now the emphasis is on price and performance.

Display space in drugstores is at a premium. Condoms, which until relatively recent times were kept under the counter, are now up in front of the register next to the ChapStick, combs, and other impulse items. Competition is keen for this exposure. Products must turn over rapidly or the space will not be allotted. Condom brands compete fiercely for peg-board or shelf space in the "family planning" section. Condoms, which were formerly considered a man's item, are now also positioned among women's personal products. Women purchase 15 to 20 percent of the condoms sold. In this environment condom manufacturers must court the buyers for exposure to customers and the customer's dollar in order to maintain or increase display space. Only as long as the major brands retain the loyalty of most of the buying public will pharmacies feature them. Any shift of consumer preference jeopardizes the producer-merchant relationship. Regardless of price or past history, merchandise must sell quickly.

Food Stores

Fifty years ago the supermarket revolutionized the sale of groceries in the U.S. Self-service all but eliminated personal contact. The package did the selling at the point of purchase. Today, supermarkets with their $237 billion in sales in 1986 comprise the largest category of mass-market retailing.[8] Foodstores continue to get bigger, yielding fewer units with ever-increasing sales. An average supermarket with its 26,000 square feet of space is three times as large as an average chain drugstore and almost half the size of a discount store. However, groceries are a high-volume, low-margin business.[9] As a result, supermarkets have gradually become one-stop shopping centers and increased their lines of higher-margin products like health and beauty aids (HBA). According to Michael Atmore (writing in *Non-Food Merchandising* magazine, May 1987), supermarkets first added condoms to their list of products in 1987 and then increased their display space based on performance.[10] Thus, supermarkets became a force in condom sales in 1987. The obvious reason is high gross margins.

Most supermarkets that sell condoms offer both grocery and drug products. There were 2,200 food/drug combination stores, representing 7 percent of the 36,100 U.S. supermarkets in operation in 1988. Their sales totaled $30.8 billion or 11.5 percent of total supermarket sales; they yielded higher sales per square foot and had a higher gross margin than other supermarkets.[11] As shown on Table 4A, in just two years food stores captured 15 percent of the retail condom business. Perhaps of greater significance to this study is the fact that Ansell and some of the other condom suppliers were able to gain on the traditional market shares of Carter-Wallace and Schmid by supplying these outlets. The rapid growth of condom demand and major product recalls by the FDA in 1987 made it difficult for the leading branded condom manufacturers to keep up with demand. When necessary, they chose to supply long-term customers first. This created an opportunity for others to fill the void in supply to the food markets.

Recent reports indicate that condom sales by supermarkets are not growing. Indeed, some store operators are becoming disenchanted with the slow rate of condom sales.

Convenience stores are a type of food outlet that seems well suited for retailing condoms. Their customer mix includes large numbers of teenagers and young adults. They are open for extended hours. (Few drugstores open before 8 A.M. or after 10 P.M.) Convenience stores generally have a 40:60 male-to-female ratio among customers. Condoms are considered traffic boosters and profit generators. They carry gross margins of 36–38 percent.[12]

Some convenience stores are leading the movement toward displaying condoms at the check-out counter, a change most food stores have been reluctant to try. Availability at check-out is considered by some to be an ideal way to increase sales of impulse items. The display of condoms in food shops is a local preference. Many operators, particularly in the Midwest and parts of the South, believe that too open a display may be offensive to many customers.

Pilferage is considered a problem by many chains. They lack the ability to track individual items because many of these low-volume stores do not have cash registers with computer hook-ups. Small items like aspirin, condoms, toothpaste, etc., are easily concealed by thieves. In order to limit stealing and avoid problems with open display, many stores are considering using vending machines to sell condoms.

Limited space is another characteristic of convenience stores. This restricts the number of items they can carry. Most offer only one brand of condoms. Since this market also began selling condoms during the tight supply period of 1987, the less well-known brands have made significant inroads in supplying convenience stores. One observer pegged convenience store sales at 8 percent of the retail condom market (see footnote 12). This seems high, and 4 percent may be more realistic.

Mass Merchandisers

Mass merchandisers, also referred to as discount stores (e.g., K-Mart, Wal-Mart, etc.) are the second largest class of mass-market retailers. With sales of $97 billion in 1986, they represent almost 27 percent of the class and about 30 percent of the stores. Most discount stores that sell condoms stock them in the HBA areas close to the feminine hygiene products and near the after-shave lotions. Many mass merchandisers also have pharmacies within the stores. Table 4E lists the mass merchandisers with pharmacies. K-Mart and Wal-Mart have the largest number of units, accounting for almost half their stores and around 88 percent of the total run by the top-ten mass merchandising chains with pharmacies. In these dual stores, the preferred spot for condoms is in plain sight near the pharmacist's counter. Discount stores have sold condoms longer than food stores and now hold 10 percent of the retail sales. The quantity and dollar sales of condoms sold by mass merchandisers have been rising steadily. These stores are not as frequently shopped as food stores, which already have captured a 50 percent larger share of the market (i.e., 15 percent). Thus, the share of condoms sold through discount stores is comparatively small.

Leveraged Buyouts

Because of the potential effects of leveraged buyouts (LBOs) on distribution channels and consequently the condom industry, they should be understood. In recent years LBOs have become common throughout American industry. Mass retailers, including food, drug, and mass merchandisers have not been immune from this activity. LBOs are seen as a way to repel takeover attempts unwanted by existing management. They are also considered a means of avoiding the scrutiny of Wall Street. The insistence on continual growth by many in the financial community is often unrealistic, yet it can threaten the positions of many managers. As a result of such pressures, overstoring has become a problem with many retail operations—as indicated by the unprofitability of 25 percent of the nation's retail real estate.

A leveraged buyout is a device whereby the firm's assets and/or cash-generating potential are offered as collateral for a loan whose proceeds are used to buy the company's outstanding shares of stock. The result is a closely or privately held firm heavily ladened with debt. With high interest obligations relative to earnings and cash flow, any unforeseen disruptions, sometimes even minor ones, can cause an organization to default (Revco's bankruptcy is an example). While exposure to such an occurrence effects all suppliers, the small size of the condom manufacturers relative to the great size of the giant retail chains using LBOs, makes them particularly vulnerable. Condom manufacturers need the high volume of sales controlled by the retailer, yet condom sales are a tiny part of a chain's total purchases. The need for cash has led some chains financed through LBOs to seek payments for "slotting" or guaranteed display space (These techniques are explained in Chapter 5).

Drug Wholesalers

The U.S. Civil War is credited with the evolution of the drug wholesaler. Before the war druggists traveled to large suppliers in the East once or twice a year to purchase chemicals and other medicinal products. After the war new territories were quickly opened and settled. Drug sales became highly competitive, and merchandise was brought directly to the retailer. Destructive competition led to emphasis on price over quality. To bring order to this business, several wholesalers formed what has since become the National Wholesale Druggists Association (NWDA) in 1876. Its purpose was to "correct excessive and unmercantile competition" and remove "evils and customers that are against good policy and sound business principle."[13]

Wholesaling grew, but it has always experienced competition from manufacturers who sell directly to retailers, thereby keeping profit margins low.

In the late 1960s, drug wholesalers began to computerize their operations in order to compete more effectively. In the early 1970s, computer links between wholesalers and manufacturers started revolutionizing the order process. Those who did not keep pace with technical progress either failed or were acquired. In 1980 there were 145 corporate members of the NWDA; by 1985 only 100 remained. Thus, the wholesalers, like the mass retailers, have been continuously consolidating. Drug wholesalers supply HBA items to food outlets as well as pharmacies. They are important links in condom distribution.

Sales Representatives

All condom manufacturers have retail sales forces, but they vary in size and the comprehensiveness of their coverage. Carter-Wallace, with a broad line of OTC products, has lower unit sales costs than the other condom manufacturers. For Carter-Wallace the cost of a sales call is spread over many products. Schmid has a narrow line and therefore is at a comparative disadvantage. (Prior to its acquisition by Carter-Wallace, Youngs had about the same unit sales costs as Schmid.) Ansell has the fewest OTC items and therefore makes the greatest use of independent representatives in order to minimize sales costs.

Most condom manufacturers use independent sales representatives for some calls. These individuals or firms usually carry lines from several manufacturers and thereby offer a wide range of merchandise. This helps keep the cost of selling low. Agents sell on a commission basis and are paid based on performance. Such firms offer a low-cost way to reach smaller or widely scattered customers. Some may also provide entry into accounts where the representative has a personal relationship with the buyer. Schmid used agents to reach many food stores which were outside their traditional marketing focus. Ansell, because of their small share of the retail market, has traditionally used commission agents. It was only during the boom period starting in 1986 that Ansell started to invest in a sales force to supplement the independents and provide a more aggressive effort. Representatives focus their efforts on high-commission, large-volume products. Therefore small-volume items, like condoms, seldom receive adequate attention. Condom manufacturers other than Carter-Wallace face the problem of weighing the costs of the various options for sales representation against the effectiveness and profit contribution of each alternative.

In addition to sales representatives, most firms have "detail" personnel. These are often part-time employees—students, housewives, etc.—who visit stores and check the merchandise on display. They fill peg-boards and shelves, straighten the displays, make certain no expired merchandise is still being offered, and clean off any dust that may have accumulated. Salespersons do their own detailing for small individual stores. Detailing is most often used to service the store locations of chains with central purchasing departments.

Vending Machines

In 1988 fifty million condoms (about 350,000 gross) were sold through vending machines in the United States. These had a retail value of around $25 million ($5 million wholesale). National Sanitary Laboratories (NSL), of Chicago, Illinois, is the largest supplier, selling 175,000–200,000 gross of condoms a year for machine vending. This equates to a market share of 50 to 60 percent. The second major supplier, Barnetts Inc., of Charlotte, North Carolina, is about 60 percent the size of NSL with sales of 100,000–120,000 gross a year. Representatives of both NSL and Barnetts claim sales are growing 10 to 20 percent a year based on opening new outlets. Most firms supplying condoms for vending machines import them from the Far East. NSL had been buying condoms from Circle Rubber until the Newark, New Jersey, plant was shut down. Their latest supplier is unknown.

Condoms sold in vending machines are currently intended to retail for $0.50 each and cost the jobber, who owns the machine and keeps it supplied, $0.10. About 20 to 30 percent of the mark-up ($0.08–$0.12 per condom) is paid to the location operator for allowing the machine in his establishment. A good location will sell 2.5–5 condoms a day per machine. This makes the income to the jobber $0.70–$1.60 per day or $250–$600 a year per machine. From this the jobber must pay all his operating expenses: automobile costs, gasoline, pilferage losses, machine repairs, etc. A condom vending machine costs $250–$300.

College campuses are among the most widely publicized locations for condom vending machines. A spokesperson for a major university was proud of selling 1,100 condoms in a year through 15 machines. Using the above values and assuming the school did not take a percentage for placing the machines in dormitories, the jobber would have grossed $440 for the year on an investment of $4,125. Considering the level of interest rates and the destructive habits of many students, the return hardly seems to justify the effort.

In spite of the above example, the sale of condoms through vending machines can be a reasonable way for a person to make a living, but it is unlikely to prove lucrative. The share of earnings received by the location operator is also small (17–60 cents per day per machine). Therefore, most proprietors allow the units on their premises more as a convenience for their patrons than for the profit. These factors lead to the conclusion that the machine vending of condoms will continue to grow, but the unattractive margins make it unlikely to become a major outlet.

Mail Order

Between 30,000 and 40,000 gross of condoms were sold through the mail during 1988. Catalogue suppliers also usually offer a wide selection of exotic clothes, adult books, and films, dildos, vibrators, etc., as well as condoms.

The largest mail-order supplier of condoms is PHE Inc., of Carrboro, North Carolina, parent company of Adam & Eve, a regular advertiser in *Playboy* and other men's magazines. This firm offers a variety of condoms including the national brands from Carter-Wallace, Schmid, and Ansell. They claim to supply 50 to 60 percent of the mail-order condoms. Adam & Eve describes their average buyer as "34–44 years old, college educated, married with children living at home, and with above average household incomes. They have spent an average of $35 per order; 30% have used major credit cards to pay for their purchases." The main attractions of buying condoms through the mail include privacy, variety, and moderate prices.

Other vendors of condoms through the mail include: Stamford Hygienic Corp., of Stamford, Connecticut, Mellow Mail, of San Rafael, California, and The Pleasure Chest, of New York, New York. This is a small, specialized market which is not likely to have a significant impact on the industry.

Social Distribution Programs

Social distribution programs are public health-social action activities which dispense condoms, as well as advice and other aids, to the public. Their purposes are to foster birth control and/or prevent the transmission of STDs, particularly AIDS. These programs take many forms and seek to place condoms into the hands of those who should use them. Teenagers and homosexual males have been priority targets. The condoms are given away free or sold on a nonprofit basis. A large number of organizations provide this service, but no single unit covers the entire market. Therefore, statistics on the size of these operations are not available. The Planned Parenthood Federation formerly bought condoms centrally and sold them to their affiliates. Unfortunately for this study, they ceased this practice in the mid–1980s and no longer have data on how many condoms are distributed through their outlets. Around 1985 the number was in the range of three to four million a year. These were all imported from the Far East. Other types of organizations which distribute condoms include hospitals, municipal health departments, colleges and universities, churches, gay organizations, etc. A best-guess places the size of these operations at 200,000–250,000 gross a year. The significances of social distribution programs to this study are: they could be outlets for manufacturers, they help develop new users, and they divert potential sales from the retail market.

Oligopsony

An oligopsony consists of a few buyers for the entire output of an industry. A better description of the condition prevailing in the retail distribution of condoms might be "overlapping monopsonies" since many retailers have a lock on access to certain customers in specific geographic markets. As a result, the retailer prevents the oligopolist from earning monopoly profits directly in the marketplace and retains the advantages for himself. This type of situation was predicted by J.K. Galbraith in 1952 as the fate of most oligopolists: "As a common rule we can rely on countervailing power to appear as a curb on economic power."[14] Shepherd, in discussing Galbraith's theory, noted that "the result could be ideal—oligopolies would achieve economies of scale and pursue innovation, but their market power would be neutralized. Strong retailers were among the units . . . Galbraith cited."[15] Shepherd went on to discuss discount retail chains as examples of firms with monopsony power. This situation is certainly descriptive of the relationships among the retailers and the condom producers. However, it would be wrong to assume that the condom industry is representative of all oligopolies. In addition, retailers do not enjoy oligopsony/monopsony power over all their suppliers. Many well-advertised branded merchandise manufacturers also have market power. Because of extensive advertising by some manufacturers, retailers are often forced by consumer demand to carry specific items. In such instances manufacturers frequently are in a position to specify the general price level.

Insights

Study of the distribution channels for condoms raises several economic issues. Most studies of oligopoly treat the manufacturers and only tangentially discuss the methods of distribution the oligopolists employ. The structure of the condom manufacturing industry cannot realistically be understood independent of the structure of the industry which controls its access to the consumer. The relative strengths of each industry determine the price structure, barriers to entry, and efficiency.

First, because the firms comprising the retail distribution channels are large in terms of financial strength, number of stores, and access to the consumer, condom manufacturers have little influence on setting consumer prices. Retailers do not simplistically mark up all items the same amount or percent over the producer's price. Prices are set on individual items in such a way as to maximize the total profit on all the merchandise sold by a store. Products that consumers buy frequently and shop for competitively carry relatively low markups and may even be sold at a loss. Income foregone in the pricing of such items is recouped by greater margins on commodities which are purchased less frequently or on impulse—such as condoms. Another factor in retail pricing is visibility: products subject to considerable publicity, as condoms were in 1987, may be priced low to advertise the store's low-price image. Many nationally advertised products carry suggested retail prices which limit the retailer's flexibility in terms of markup.

Surprisingly, location has little bearing on the price of condoms. Often merchants have been observed pricing a box of condoms high even though there is another store a few doors away selling identical merchandise for considerably less.

Second, drugstores are still the largest outlet for condoms in the United States. Therefore, many of the historical relationships and traditional price levels have continued. Professional buyers will not permit sizeable price increases that cannot be justified based on costs, but they have not tried to force prices down by promoting less well known brands. Because the demand for condoms is price inelastic, retailers have little incentive to employ such tactics with this product line. While virtually every industry has some consumers who buy based on price, they represent a very small portion of the condom users.

Third, the size and strength of the retail distributors favor the continuance of an oligopolistic structure for condom manufacturing. It is to the retailer's advantage to perpetuate this pattern of industry organization. A limited number of well-known brands keeps turnover high, makes price control easier, and limits the necessity of increasing the number of stock-keeping units.

Fourth, when food stores started to sell condoms in 1987, this opened an important new channel for reaching the consumer. However, when the major brands were unable to supply enough merchandise, food stores stocked other brands, particularly Ansell's Lifestyles. As a result, food stores now account for 15 percent of retail condom sales, and the Ansell brand gained significantly more market share.

Food stores opened new avenues of exposure to the consumer and provided an opportunity for a formerly minor competitor to weaken to some extent the entrenched positions of Schmid and Carter-Wallace. This illustrates how circumstances more than competitive action often affect the structure of an industry. It is still too early to predict how far and how fast change will affect the condom industry. Whether the change is rapid or slow, continuous or intermittent is unimportant for purposes of this presentation. The main point is that while the established condom manufacturers are presently in a strong position, it is capable of erosion. The structure of the industry is likely to evolve into a more competitive form if the market grows.

Fifth, because of the dependence of the condom manufacturers on access to the consumer, they are vulnerable to pressure from the large retail chains. If a chain gets into financial trouble and puts pressure on its suppliers, they could force short-term concessions with possible long-term impact on the condom industry. The condom manufacturers are too weak to resist strongly. The industry is too small for any concessions to one retailer not to be noticed by the others. The potential for such a move is to lower the price level, the profitability of all the condom manufacturers, and their capability to continue to promote the use of condoms.

Sixth, efforts to make the purchase of condoms easier and less embarrassing through drug and food stores may have reduced the attractions of condom vending machines and mail-order catalogs. Further increasing the availability of condoms may result in greater inefficiencies in the distribution chain and lower the incentive for the traditional outlets to promote condom sales. Confidentiality is no longer a strong reason to use inanimate outlets like vending machines and the mail. Thus, little growth is expected through these outlets.

Seventh, social distribution programs are growing. These operations encourage new users and thereby promote the general welfare of the population. They help increase the total demand for condoms but divert sales from retail outlets and build no brand loyalty. An obvious strategy would be to provide branded condoms through social action programs. This would trigger objections from the retailers since there would be no incentive for persons to pay the full retail price when they could get the same products free or at minimum cost. Also there is a stigma attached to publicly dispensed products; many recipients believe such products are in some way inferior to commercially purchased merchandise.

Eighth, the main channels through which condoms reach the consumer comprise a strong oligopsony and in certain instances may include regional monopsonies. It is the strength of these buying groups which maintains the oligopoly in condom manufacturing and the administered transaction price to the retailer. (Unfortunately, no economic literature on buyer concentration was uncovered which is relevant to this particular situation. Writers on the subject of oligopsony/monopsony such as Bookings,[16] Just,[17] Lustgarten,[18,19] McIntosh,[20] Guth, Swartz, and Whitcomb[21,22] have focused primarily on manufacturers purchasing raw materials or labor and not on retailers buying branded products. Galbraith is the one researcher uncovered in this study who reported some insights into the development of retail monopsonies.)

Chapter 5

The Competitive Situation

Overview

The way products are sold is important in defining the type of competition which most clearly describes an industry structure. In order for an industry to be considered an oligopoly, not only must few producers control a major portion of demand, but the means through which they compete are also important. In the oligopolistic portion of imperfect competition, prices are comparatively rigid and nonprice methods of rivalry predominate.

This chapter describes the relative retail market positions of the condom manufacturers, discusses prices at both the consumer and wholesale levels, explores the influence of prices on demand, and focuses on the nonprice techniques used to gain or retain market share. Each factor is investigated in relation to its contribution toward the oligopolistic structure of this industry and barriers to entry. The scope includes past practices, the current situation, and emerging actions which may have implications for the future.

Market Shares

Together Carter-Wallace and Schmid Laboratories accounted for 74.3 percent of the retail dollar sales of condoms in the United States during 1988. This is down from the 83.7 percent share they held jointly in 1986. Reportedly, both firms lost some sales due to an inability to supply all the condoms ordered in 1987. As a result, Ansell and the other smaller firms captured improved market positions, particularly among food stores. Food outlets, which only started to sell condoms in 1987, now account for 15 percent of the market.

Table 5A lists the retail dollar sales of condoms by supplier for the years 1982 through 1988. Of particular note is the 50 percent increase in demand experienced in 1987 compared with 1986. Between 1982 and 1985 the market averaged a 3 percent a year increase. In 1986, when the AIDS situation started to be publicly recognized, market demand grew by 5

Table 5A. Estimated U.S. Retail Sales of Condoms 1982–88[1]
(All Values in $Millions)

Year	*Ansell*	*Carter-Wallace*	*Schmid Labs.*	*Others*[2]	*Total*
1982	$ 4.6	$ 58.9	$49.3	$19.3	$132.1
1983	5.5	58.7	49.8	17.0	131.0
1984	6.0	61.7	50.3	17.3	135.3
1985	5.8	67.1	53.3	18.3	144.5
1986	5.3	69.8	57.7	19.5	152.3
1987	18.0	102.1	68.1	40.0	228.5
1988	19.4	109.8	73.1	43.7	246.0

1. Includes latex and skin condoms; necessary data to permit separating out skin condoms were not available for all years.
2. Includes all condoms sold through vending machines.

Source: The estimates in this table were computed from data contained in published articles, data on retail sales and warehouse stock movements, and interviews with knowledgeable individuals active in the industry. Therefore, they reflect the writer's research and are not known to closely follow the findings of any other individuals or organizations.

---

percent. In light of these figures, it is easy to understand how manufacturers could be caught unprepared for the jump in 1987 demand. Unfortunately, the market has not continued to grow at this pace. The 1988 gain over 1987 was only 7.7 percent.

Also of competitive importance is the fact that in 1987 Ansell more than doubled its market share and other small suppliers gained position. As shown in Table 5B, Carter-Wallace managed to keep up with the market growth fairly well, losing only 1 percent of its market share. Schmid Laboratories suffered the largest loss with a 21.4 percent drop in its market share. As part of the London International Group (LIG), which operates condom manufacturing plants around the world, Schmid would probably have been well positioned to supply the quantities required if the boom in demand had not been worldwide. Unfortunately, LIG's other plants were also experiencing unusually high demand and were unable to provide extra condoms for the U.S. market. Thus, as new outlets opened, Schmid was unable to fill their orders. Some of the demand at the wholesale level was artificial, brought on by overordering in response to a tight supply situation.

In spite of recent market shifts, Carter-Wallace and Schmid Laboratories continue to provide the bulk of the condoms for retail sales. When Ansell's share is included, these firms hold 82.2 percent of the market. The condom industry is clearly an example of dominance by a few producers with little actual product differentiation.

Table 5B. Market Shares of U.S. Retail Condom Market 1982–88 (Based on Data Listed in Table 5A) Carter-Schmid

Year	*Ansell*	*Wallace*	*Labs.*	*Others*[2]	*Total*
1982	$3.4	$44.2	37.2%	14.6%	100.0%
1983	4.2	43.6	38.2	13.1	100.0
1984	4.4	45.6	37.2	12.8	100.0
1985	4.0	46.4	36.9	12.7	100.0
1986	3.5	45.8	37.9	12.8	100.0
1987	7.9	44.8	29.8	17.5	100.0
1988	7.9	44.6	29.7	17.8	100.0

Source: These percentages were calculated from the estimates shown on Table 5A.

The Product

There is little differentiation among condoms from the manufacturers in the United States. The physical properties (tensile strength and ultimate elongation) of the rubber are defined by A.S.T.M. specification D 3492–83. The dimensional limits and quality inspection requirements are also listed in this specification. Variations within the allowed limits are small. The substantive differences between products include shapes, the presence or absence of lubricants, and the presence or absence of spermicides. Condoms can be straight-sided, contoured, ribbed or smooth. They can be blunt-ended or have a reservoir tip. They can be dry or carry a lubricant. The lubricants include "dry" silicone oils, wet jellies, and dry powders. (Petroleum-based lubricants cannot be used because they degrade the rubber.) Spermicides, usually nonoxonol-9, lubricate as well as protect. (Some specialty condoms are made with various appendages, bumps, etc. These products are usually sold through "sex shops" or by mail order. They represent a very small market and are not included in this study.)

The San Francisco AIDS Foundation published a *Consumers Guide to Condoms*[1] in 1987 which was reprinted in *Contraceptive Technology 1988–1989*. It provides a comprehensive description of the choices of branded contraceptives available. My own observations, while not based on as extensive a survey, closely parallel these findings. As shown on Table 5C, there is little difference among condom choices. Most have reservoir ends and are lubricated. At the time these observations were made, less than 20 percent of the brand variations were spermicidally lubricated. This is significant because of the extra protection these condoms appear to provide against STDs. Sperm ejaculated into spermicidally lubricated condoms are quickly inactivated. Moreover, recent tests have shown that nonoxonol-9 kills the AIDS and other STD viruses.

Table 5C. Survey of the Properties Used to Differentiate Condoms

No. of products compared	55
No. with reservoir ends	51
No. with lubrication	47
No. containing a spermicide	10
No. claiming to be ribbed	8

Source: This information was gathered from data on packages of latex condoms in late 1987. Only products believed to be made in the U.S. were included.

Thickness is a property that has received considerable attention as manufacturers seek ways to differentiate relatively uniform products. A.S.T.M. D 3492–83 specifies thickness limits of 0.03mm to 0.09mm. Most condoms in the United States are in the 0.04–0.06mm range. Japanese manufacturers are promoting their 0.03mm thick condoms as providing greater sensitivity. Ansell offers the "Lifestyles Extra Strength" condom, which is thicker and is claimed to be 20 to 25 percent stronger. The term "stronger" is somewhat misleading for condoms. One might assume they mean abrasion resistance since sexual intercourse involves a rubbing action. But tensile strength is the property that is measured, a strength which may not be meaningful. The unstated, but implied, use for the extra-strength product is for anal sex. Clinicians have pointed out that anal sex may put more stress on condoms than penile-vaginal sex and thereby increase the risk of breakage. But most failure problems associated with condoms have been traced to improper use rather than to deficiencies in the product.

Brands

With little difference in products, condom producers differentiate their output through brand identification. As mentioned previously, the Trojan brand of Carter-Wallace is synonomous with condoms for many individuals. How Youngs, the former owners, built the Trojan name has already been described. At this time it is the dominant brand in the United States. Carter-Wallace offers a complete line of condoms and uses the Trojan label on every item in the line.

Schmid Laboratories, with the second largest market share, sells its latex condoms under four names: Sheik, Ramses, Excita, and Koromex. Schmid markets skin sheaths under the Fourex brand. Thus Schmid's brand identity is spread over a variety of products, complicating advertising efforts and diluting the impact of the firm's image in this industry.

Ansell uses the Lifestyles, Prime, and Rough Rider labels. Most of their

Table 5D. Retail Condom Prices
($ Per Box of 12)

Product	*High*	*Low*	*Range*	*Average*
Ramses Extra	$8.79	$3.59	$5.20	$6.44
Sheik Elite	6.65	2.79	3.86	4.84
Excita 12s	8.65	3.49	5.16	6.46
Trojan Plus	8.95	3.09	5.89	5.51
Trojan Enz & Lube	6.39	2.79	3.60	4.68
Trojan Ribbed	8.49	3.09	5.40	5.48

These data were based on prices recorded from merchandise in 29 stores in various parts of the country in 1986. A spot check in December 1988 indicated that the information is still a reasonable representation of the market. The brands were chosen because they are products of the two leading firms, Carter-Wallace and Schmid. Trojan Enz & Lube is the most popular condom variety in the U.S.

---

advertising and promotion is focused on Lifestyles. Circle Rubber's brands include Saxon, Pleasehers, Embracehers, and Gold Circle. National Sanitary Laboratories's products use the names Sunrise, Touch, Arouse, Contracept Plus, and Manform.

Manufacturers usually market several varieties of condoms (e.g., tipped, lubricated, etc.) under each brand name. Brand name proliferation developed as producers sought to enter different market segments. For example, Schmid's Koromex condom was intended to appeal to women by association with Schmid's line of diaphragms and spermicides. Carter-Wallace is the only manufacturer using a single brand and therefore is able to concentrate all marketing efforts on promoting the Trojan brand.

Prices

Price theory is indefinite in predicting market conduct and performance in most oligopolistic industries. There are many competitive options and the success of each relies interdependently on the responses of rivals. As each seller seeks to increase market share and profits, competitors monitor his actions and quickly counter any moves that may be at their expense. While adhering to these general rules of competitive behavior, the U.S. condom industry exhibits a different situation relative to prices.

Analysis of prices for the condom industry must be conducted separately at the retail and producer levels. The prices charged by manufacturers have only minor influence on the prices charged to consumers. Retail condom prices differ widely for the same product as illustrated by the data in Table 5D. For individual items the top retail prices have been as much as $5.89 (almost 50 cents a condom) more than the low price charged for the same product by a different merchant. Obviously these prices were not set based on manufacturing costs or even the prices charged by manufacturers. The large producers have national price lists, and shipping charges are insignificant for condoms.

The retail prices reflect:

1. Relative price inelasticity. Consumers would not buy substantially more condoms at a lower price. Even at the highest prices listed (75 cents per condom) the unit cost of a condom is low. Thus, few customers shop for condoms based on price. Confidence in the integrity of the product appears to be the prime concern.

2. Condoms are often purchased on impulse, further limiting the chance that consumers will seek the lowest price.

3. Retailers who price condoms very low often use them to advertise the low-price image of their stores.

4. Because the price of condoms is low (less than $1 per unit) and because of the reassurance an established brand provides the consumer in terms of protection, there has been comparatively little switching among brands by those who buy condoms regularly.

The wide variations in retail prices also reflect the high margins available on condoms. Not even the retailers with the lowest prices are selling at a loss. Typically, condoms are marked up 150 percent for a 60 percent gross margin. Individual retailers adjust their prices above or below this norm depending on their merchandising policies. Retail pricing depends on a variety of factors including the type of goods, store image, profit desired, customer demand, competition, and supplier policies.[2] As Davidson, Sweeney, and Stampfl expressed it: "at the heart of the retailer's pricing question is perceived value by the consumer."[3]

In spite of retail pricing policies, condom manufacturers face a "kinked" demand curve. Power rests with the retail chains at the wholesale level. As shown by Ansell's gains in market share in 1987, when retailers (in this case supermarkets) stocked their shelves with an alternative brand, it sold. (Apparently these sales were primarily to persons who either had not purchased condoms before or had not yet developed a brand preference.) Retailers have their own profit-maximizing motives. Profit is a function of both the markup and stock turnover (i.e., how quickly the product is sold). Established brands sell faster, reflecting the consumers' preferences.

Control of exposure to the consumer provides merchants with the ability to keep manufacturers from raising their prices. Downside discipline is enforced by other manufacturers who will quickly match or better price cuts to prevent a rival from gaining a competitive advantage. Since demand is inelastic, total sales are unlikely to increase based on lower prices. It would be more realistic for retailers to increase their stocks in response to a price cut either in anticipation that the cut will be temporary or to encourage other manufacturers also to reduce prices. The long-term effect would simply be an exchange of purchases now for purchases later. This is a neutral move in terms of total volume because manufacturers have no way of changing the inelastic final demand. Thus, condom producers are caught in a relatively rigid system with only narrow flexibility with regard to pricing.

The producer price level for condoms is set to yield positive profits only at outputs and sales volumes that represent large shares of the total market. This practice denies potential new entrants the option of entering the business and expanding gradually. The losses incurred at low levels of output combined with the difficulty of taking market share away from established producers makes entry by a new domestic manufacturer exceedingly difficult.

The way the price of condoms at the producer level was established is discussed more fully under a later section of this chapter dealing with the "kinked demand curve." However, at this point it is important to recognize that condom prices are:

- Administered or set to produce profits at a reasonable (normal) level of output for the established manufacturers and to deter the entry of new competitors. The prices are not the result of the action of supply and demand.

- The result of the historical development of the oligopoly structure of the condom industry. Structural rigidities are necessary to maintain administered prices. The existence of collusion or price leadership by the dominant producer are the most frequently cited examples. The price rigidity in the condom industry comes from different sources. In the first half of the twentieth century, the so-called little Comstock laws led to the formation of the condom oligopoly, thereby setting the stage for administered prices. More recently the evolution of a strong retailing oligopsony has continued this pricing arrangement.

- Inelastic at the consumer level, which makes it impractical to try to increase sales based on price competition.

Reported financial costs may differ among manufacturers. Such variations are more likely to be a function of bookkeeping preferences or variations in sales or administrative costs than fundamental differences in manufacturing costs. The processes are very similar; raw materials costs are comparable; and when the plants are operated at the high throughputs for which they were designed, the fixed overhead charges will be low on a unit basis. Cost differences are more likely to reflect variations in sales, marketing, and advertising costs.

Condom manufacturers rely on the preferences of buyers to pull their products through the store. However, with three leading suppliers, each must remain aware of the others' pricing policies. While it is difficult for unknown brands to break into the market, consumer brand switching among the well-recognized items is much easier because of confidence in the established brands. This gives retailers the option of playing one supplier against the others. With national price lists and so few competitors, advantages are usually sought through nonprice competition.

Advertising

Advertising methods can be separated into point-of-purchase (POP) promotion and media advertising. Both are relatively new to the condom industry. For most of their history, condoms were considered products which should not be talked about. Druggists kept supplies in drawers or under the counter. Therefore, no promotion or advertising was needed or could be used. In late 1986 and 1987, condoms became news when the surgeon general of the United States endorsed them. On the front pages of newspapers, on news broadcasts, and in classrooms, educators, medical experts, and public officials urged people to use condoms. The scourge of AIDS terrified people as the fear of STDs like syphilis or gonorrhea never had. Antibiotics can help with other STDs, but there is no cure for AIDS. Unfortunately, the surge of free publicity died down and with it the growth of the condom business.

Condoms are now openly displayed in stores, usually in what has come to be known as "the family planning section." This section often consists of a display rack set on the retail counter or a section of peg-board where the products of several vendors are displayed. Great emphasis is placed on product packaging. Bright colors and attractive designs are used to catch the consumer's eye. Packages are designed not only to attract but also not to offend. Gays, for example, are not receptive to photos of heterosexual couples embracing. Many people prefer neutral designs which do not scream the contents of the package. Some people prefer not to flaunt their purchase of condoms. Products designed to appeal to women may not be effective for males; a condom must be worn by a male, and he could be turned off by a feminine-looking container.

In addition to increasing the visual impact of their brands, condom manufacturers also provide educational materials. These are intended to inform consumers about the properties and correct use of condoms, to warn about the dangers of AIDS and STDs, and to enhance the image of the manufacturer as a serious supplier of a device on which the user can rely. Media advertising has been a controversial topic for condom manufacturers. The leaders would prefer that there were no condom ads. Their reasons include:

1. Increased costs.

2. Don't know how to use ads effectively.

3. Lack confidence that advertising will expand the market.

4. A good ad campaign by an unknown brand might effect current market shares.

In 1987 Ansell led media advertising by condom manufacturers. On television and in print media, they published an ad created by Jerry Della Femina which dramatically brought home the condom message. It featured a young woman making the statement, "I'll do a lot for love, but I'm not ready to die for it." This ad apparently offended many people, but it did what ads are supposed to do: it got people's attention, put the Lifestyles brand in front of the public's eyes, and was both memorable and controversial. The advertisement is no longer used. In February 1987 Della Femina, Travisano, and Partners resigned as Ansell's advertising agency.[4]

Other condom producers have chosen more subtle approaches. Schmid Laboratories, for example, ran an ad featuring a father's advice to his son at school. One of Carter-Wallace's ads featured the headline, "Very often the best contraceptive for a woman is the one for a man."[5] Lifestyles has recently taken a lighter, somewhat comical approach.

Most condom ads now appear in magazines. Print messages are less expensive and can be more informative. In spite of a dramatic change from the sensational ads that appeared in "adult" publications before 1986, many publishers still refuse to carry condom ads. This was a controversial point in 1987, but judging from the lack of recent comments few publishers or manufacturers seem to care anymore.

There is no reliable information available concerning the effectiveness of condom advertising. Reportedly, in 1987 condom manufacturers spent more than $23 million on ads. This was more than 10 percent of retail sales or over 20 percent of producer sales, a sizeable commitment. The market grew over 7 percent in 1988 but has since flattened. In 1988 most condom producers were expected to spend considerably more on ads than they did in 1987. Judging from the significant decline in available ads, it is doubtful these estimates were fulfilled. Unless the demand for condoms expands greatly, it would be hard to justify large promotional expenditures. All signs indicate that condom producers believe point-of-purchase presentations are the most cost-effective means of merchandising. Forms of nonprice competition other than advertising are being emphasized.

Nonprice Competition

Nonprice competition is the most effective means of rivalry open to an oligopolist. Point-of-purchase and media advertising have already been covered, There are a number of other techniques directed toward the consumer or the merchant which are considered to be "nonprice" in that they do not affect the list price of condoms. The result of many of these actions is at least a temporary lower cost to the buyer.

Programs designed to influence consumer purchases include:

1. Coupons on the packages which provide discounts on future purchases.

2. Bonus packs which include free condoms with the purchase. For example: three free condoms and a carrying case with the purchase of one dozen.

3. Buy one, get one free promotions (i.e., two for the price of one).

4. Coupons for discount which are included as part of the POP display material. (Whether or not these coupons always directly benefit the consumer or the retailer uses the coupons to lower his costs is difficult to determine. The cost is the same to the producer. However, if the customer does not benefit, the intention of stimulating sales and attracting new users is subverted.)

The incentives offered to the retailers are more aggressive. Most involve price cuts without changing list prices. These inducements to purchase include:

1. A rebate paid for guaranteed shelf or peg space; this involves a return of a percentage of the sales revenue to the merchant as a bonus for displaying the merchandise.

2. Special deductions from invoice prices to promote the sale of individual stock keeping units (skus).

3. "Bill-backs" to offset the cost of advertising by retailers (i.e., the merchant invoices the manufacturer for monies spent to advertise his product).

4. An introductory allowance to induce the retailer to start selling the product (new outlets) or to introduce a new item or size through an existing outlet.

5. Slotting allowances; This is a fee the manufacturer pays the retailer to list his or her product as approved for purchase.

6. Delayed invoicing; under this arrangement, retailers are not billed immediately after shipment, and often not until most of the products have been sold.

Most of the above incentives are common in the sale of other health and beauty aids as well as condoms.

Slotting allowances have become more common in recent years. About 20 years ago, several manufacturers initiated slotting allowances as a way to limit the shelf space allotted to smaller vendors.[6] Established producers used this method to discourage competition. It has only recently become an active competitive strategy in the condom industry. Retailers view slotting fees as a way to offset the expenses for warehousing and planograming products. However, the practice is not restricted to new products. Some established condom manufacturers are offering to pay slotting fees to get and keep prime display space. Such space is essential to maintain volume and expand sales. Regular condom users switch brands infrequently. Thus, the base demands for Trojans and Schmid are likely to change slowly with the aging of the population. The competition is for the new user. Easy availability is the key to capturing this market segment. Therefore, condom manufacturers view slotting as a means to maintain consumer exposure and deny access to new brands. This could be an important barrier to entry for the condom business.

The Kinked Demand Curve

Condom manufacturers face a kinked demand curve of a type that has been considered by some economists to be the primary theory of price in oligopolistic industries. Other economists challenge the validity of this theory of pricing. Demand is usually depicted as a straight line showing, except for completely inelastic circumstances, sales increase over some range as price decreases. A kinked demand curve has a vertical section indicating that changes in price do not result in shifts in sales volume. (Some graphs of kinked curves show a point where demand switches from an elastic to an inelastic slope. However, for condoms, the demand curve is dominated by a vertical section mirroring the inelastic consumer demand curve faced by the retailers.) The ends of this vertical section are connected to sloped segments. The rate of incline on the high end is visualized as being more elastic than it is at the lower end.

Economists seem to favor assuming a kinked demand configuration when inflation is low and they have difficulty explaining lack of price movement. The condom industry in the United States provides an example of the existence of conditions under which a kinked demand curve offers the most plausible explanation of the observed situation, albeit under a different set of circumstances than those usually postulated in the literature.

Most discussions of oligopolistic pricing start with the assumption that the oligopolist has market power and therefore a strong influence on the establishment of its selling prices. But market power is a relative not an absolute trait. Condom manufacturers have market power in the sense that they have a loyal following of customers for their branded products. Condom users do not switch brands very easily provided that their preferred product can be purchased conveniently. But the producer's ability to exercise this marketing strength is counterbalanced by the oligopsonistic retail distribution channel which controls access to the consumer. Facing a price-inelastic consumer demand curve, the retailers have the ability to set final prices without a direct relationship to the prices paid to the manufacturers. The oligopsonist structure of the retail chains transfers much of the usually assumed oligopoly market power to the store operators. Because of the large number of stores run by each of the largest chains, these retailers have virtual monopoly power over the exposure of certain products, like condoms, to the consumer. The condom industry generates too few dollars for the manufacturers to afford advertising expenditures of the magnitude it would take to draw sales consistently through the retail stores (i.e., to force the retailers to carry their product because it is being demanded by consumers). Condoms represent too low a proportion of the retailer's total sales and profit dollars for the manufacturers to be able to exert a strong influence on the store buyers. As a result, the retail chain purchasing agent generally controls the price paid to the condom manufacturer.

The prevailing producer price level for condoms evolved from historical pricing and a marketing strategy set by Youngs and Schmid during the period before the retail drug and food industries developed into an oligopsony. The evidence suggests a desire to establish a price which would discourage the entry of new competitors. A price level was found which at some normally achieveable volume of sales for the established producers would be above their costs but would be below prices at which potential competitors could reasonably expect to enter the market and earn positive profits. By setting prices equal to their average cost (including sales, general and administrative expenses, plus manufacturing costs and a minimum acceptable return on investment) at a volume which is a significant share of the total market demand, the established condom producers discourage new entrants and open an opportunity to share among themselves monopoly profits during periods when demand exceeds this threshold volume. (This should become evident in Chapter 9 where the profits for the condom industry are presented and discussed.) Sylos-Labini, Modigliani, and Bain represent economic theorists whose formulations of limit-pricing theories point to the existence of a kink in the demand curve.[7]

While the large retail firms have the power to force significant price reductions on the condom industry, they lack incentives to do so. Consumer demand is price inelastic: consequently the retailer may set any price he/she deems appropriate. Retailers compute their income based on markup times turnover. This makes it advantageous for them to keep the condom manufacturers profitable enough to maintain an image with the public that encourages sales. If the price is forced too low, it might discourage the producers from developing new or new-appearing products which are "fresh" and appealing to the consumer (the FDA requirements will not tolerate deterioration of quality), strengthen the position of foreign-based producers, and possibly lead to retail price competition. There is no advantage to the retailer in a large number of variations of a comparatively slow-moving product category. More brands, each with smaller market shares, would require additional inventories and extra purchasing and administrative attention. The added inventories could be composed of more condoms or simply more stockkeeping units (skus). In either case the handling costs rise, control becomes more cumbersome, and paperwork increases. Also more skus require more shelf space and would most likely lead to slower turnover due to longer periods between the sale of each item. With fewer, well-known brands, the items on display sell more rapidly.[8] It is to the retailer's advantage to maintain the current industry structure with regard to condoms (i.e., a few well-established suppliers with the retailers in control relative to the prices they pay for condoms and the prices they can charge customers).

With the retail merchants holding such a powerful position, it might seem that there is no upper portion to the demand curve (i.e., no kink exists). But for condoms an area of declining demand with higher prices does potentially exist. Brand loyalty and habit buying are strong among condom users. Regular customers seek their usual brand. Retailers may be reluctant to continue to stock a brand for which they must pay a higher price than competitive products, but they also do not want to alienate customers. Therefore, a rational response to a challenge to prevailing prices by a condom manufacturer would be to decrease the number of that manufacturer's skus on display. This would make it more difficult, but not impossible, for consumers to locate the item at all times. Such a practice would gradually discourage consumers, make the attraction of new users less likely, and eventually reduce the producer's market share. In addition, the allocation of more display space to competing products will, at least over time, increase the market position of these items at the expense of the rebellious supplier. Exposure of products to the consumer is essential to the sale of condoms. For condoms, demand is more likely to decline for a manufacturer due to the enforcement of industry price discipline rather than any consumer response to higher prices.

While it has not been tested, there is a price level at which consumption will increase (the extent of the demand increase is the part that is not defineable). These increased sales may only apply to one brand over another or to all condoms. It is conceivable that the price may fall so low that organizations or individuals with an interest in the social effects of the nonuse of condoms may take steps to provide the public with condoms free of charge. Whatever the circumstances or extent, there is a price at which some increase in sales will occur. If the product is priced low enough, increased wastage alone should raise the need for more units. The crucial question is whether the price at which the demand curve moves from the vertical is sufficient to make it worthwhile for condom manufacturers to continue to operate. Another example of how the condom industry confirms the generally accepted theory of the kinked demand curve is that, for condoms, the lower tail is unlikely to be more elastic than the higher-price nonvertical segment. Demand for condoms has proven to be hard to change. While there is bound to be some price effect at some point, it is difficult to visualize realistic circumstances which would make the demand price elasticity 1.0 or greater.

The theoretical demand configuration facing condom manufacturers follows a path similar to one Paul Sweezy[9] in the United States and R.L. Hall and C.J. Hitch[10] in the United Kingdom described as "kinked" and considered representative of an oligopolistic situation. The deficiency of both the Sweezy and Hitch-Hall papers lies in their omission of insight as to how the prevailing price level was attained. Hitch-Hall concluded "We cannot say precisely what this price will be." Sweezy reported: "Generally speaking there may be any number of price-output combinations which constitute equilibriums in the sense that, *ceteris paribus*, there is no tendency for the oligopolist to move away from them. But which of these combinations will be actually established in practice, depends upon the history of the case."[11] Sylos-Labini developed a theoretical rationale for determining the price in an oligopoly kinked demand situation based on a Walrasian approach with prix crie au hasard.[12] Sylos-Labini found that "the price tends to settle at a level immediately above the entry-preventing price of the least efficient firms which it is to the advantage of the largest and most efficient firms to let live. The elements of price determination are the following: (a) the absolute size of the market; (b) the elasticity of demand; (c) the technologies; (d) the price of the variable factors and of machines, which together with the technologies, determine the total average costs of the firms."[13] Each of the items postulated theoretically by these economists is confirmed by observation of the condom industry (i.e., the market price developed as a result of past history based on the market size, elasticity of demand, cost factors and competitive interplay [prix crie au hasard]). This led to the establishment of a steady price at a level which discourages the entry of new producers. One new factor revealed in this study, which was not uncovered in a search of prior analyses of the kinked demand curve, is the lack of access to the final consumer by condom producers. This lack of access is the structural rigidity which forestalls effective price competition.

It is now appropriate to expand the analysis to consider the ways the market situation in the condom industry adheres to and/or differs from the explanation of oligopolistic pricing offered by the post–Keynesian economists. W. Semmler summarized the post–Keynesian positions in his book *Competition, Monopoly, and Differential Profit Rates.*[14] Information taken from Semmler's chapter on "Empirical Evidence on Industrial and Corporate Pricing" is used here as a basis for comparison.

Semmler observed that "according to post–Keynesian authors, in oligopolistic industries price decisions are subject to great uncertainty because of interdependent reaction . . . big firms . . . will not change prices frequently. When demand falls, the adjustment will be made by lowering production and less by cutting prices." Generally this observation fits the condom industry and the kinked demand curve. The fact that prices change infrequently can be credited to the fact that consumer demand for condoms is insensitive to price changes. Except for the unusual circumstances in late 1986 and all of 1987, condom demand generally has kept pace with changes in the number of persons within the sexually active age bracket of the population.

The established producer price level in the condom industry fits the entry-preventing price strategy which Semmler attributes to authors like Bain, Sylos-Labini, Modigliani, and Baron. Under this theory oligopolistic enterprises set "prices above their costs but below prices at which potential competitors could enter the market and earn positive profits . . . their prices depend on many factors." The available evidence suggests that this aptly describes the pricing strategy of condom manufacturers. For condom manufacturers the most significant price determinants are the economies of scale at an achievable volume of sales which represents a significant market share. The authors that Semmler cited generally acknowledged that price changes are due to shifts in the cost of production and not changes in supply and demand. However, only industrywide cost changes lead to acceptable price increases in the condom industry. Cost or profitability problems of individual firms are unlikely to trigger positive responses on the part of retailers or competitors. When costs increase across the industry all oligopolists seek the same boost in price while at the same time using a rationale recognized as justified by the oligopsonists.

A substantial positive shift in demand could lead to inadequate supplies of merchandise. Conceivably, this could trigger price increases. Condom manufacturers have usually been unwilling, however, to let a short supply situation exist for very long. This is because of the opportunities to earn monopoly profits at high production levels, the ease of adding incremental manufacturing capability, and the danger of attracting added competition, particularly off-shore producers.

One of the factors in maintaining stable prices that is seldom mentioned is the importance of avoiding uncertainty in the marketplace. Consumers, chain store-buyers, planners, store clerks, manufacturers, etc. — all prefer to plan purchases, profits, strategies, etc., under well-ordered, predictable conditions. Modern business enterprises have built-in rigidities which do not respond well to frequent changes. Corporate employees are often unprepared to deal with situations in flux. These internal structural needs may have as much or more to do with the reluctance to change prices as the adjustments in factor costs or shifts in demand. Thus, while manufacturers might prefer to maintain margins which provide a minimum return on invested capital, they do not raise prices in an attempt to keep the level of earnings up when sales fall. Likewise, they do not cut prices when demand rises to a level where manufacturers are enjoying greater-than-normal profits. Most firms adopt a policy of reasonable accommodation to short-run situations rather than continual adjustment. As Alfred Kahn pointed out in his article on "Market Power Inflation,"[15] "Customers are typically more upset by frequent changing, than by stable prices, and sellers who are in a position to worry about customers' goodwill and to act on the basis of that concern are likely to behave accordingly."

Theories linking pricing decisions to a firm's desire to provide funds for future expansion fit the condom industry only indirectly. The condom manufacturers have little control over the transaction price, which makes such a planned strategy impractical. Except for the surge in demand that occurred in 1987, the U.S. condom industry has historically grown so slowly that there was little need for additional capacity. However, as identified by James Clifton in his article "Competition and the Evolution of the Capitalist Mode of Production,"[16] "It is not so much the ability of the firm to maintain existing shares of given commodities in given industries that is essential to its competitiveness vis-à-vis other firms that are highly developed. Rather it is the ability to maintain its share of the value of the economic surplus and, consequently, its own rate of expansion vis-à-vis other firms that is the criterion of competitiveness." Thus, profits generated in the condom industry are used to help finance growth in other segments of the firm that offer brighter growth prospects. Dr. Edward J. Nell, in his paper "Steady Prices in an Unsteady World,"[17] developed a model which incorporates all of the uses of "surplus" funds by the corporation into a formula for determining prices. While such applications of cash flows and their necessity for the growth and continued health of the corporation are well understood at the corporate level, most times these are translated into simplified mark-up rules for use by the price setters. Nell's contribution was to make these actions explicit and to directly tie the price and policy decisions. He has enhanced our understanding of the price mechanism and provided a basis for improved pricing strategies. Revenue, the product of price and the quantity sold, is the source of all cash. Since the quantity demanded is generally dependent on the price, price is the mechanism by which the funds for growth are generated. It matters little that these funds may be used to expand product lines other than those from which they originated.

George Stigler, in his article on "The Kinked Oligopoly Demand Curve and Rigid Prices,"[18] pointed out the difficulty in obtaining transaction prices and the unreliability of quoted prices. The condom industry provides verification of the inappropriateness of relying on list prices. However, because of the small size of the condom market and the strength of the oligopsonistic retailers, it is possible to develop fairly reliable estimates of average transaction prices. The competitive interplay among comparatively few buyers and sellers make transaction prices more stable than reported prices in the U.S. condom industry. Manufacturers are free to set list prices, but any amounts over the generally accepted transaction prices are returned through a series of discounts, allowances, and give-backs.

Dr. Stigler in his analysis found fault with the concept that "The kink is a barrier to changes in prices that will increase profits," and he makes a very plausible case for his skepticism in the industries he studies. However, in his analysis the barrier was considered a barrier "of their (the oligopolist's) own fabrication." This does not fit the condom industry. For condoms the kink is due to the combined effects of a price inelastic consumer demand curve from which the manufacturer is insulated by the oligopsony powers of the retailers. The number of practical tactical options open to the condom manufacturers is limited in such a small industry, with the benefits heavily weighted to the advantage of the buyer (retailer) and not the supplier. The mechanism that maintains the price is a process of mutual accommodation whereby the oligopolists and the oligopsonists act in ways that preserve the status quo, serving the long-term interests of both groups.

Few, if any, enterprises can put meaningful numbers to the demand curves for their products. As William Baumol observed, "Demand functions . . . are . . . abstract . . . marked by an aura of unreality . . . a demand curve can never be observed directly with any degree of confidence because by the time we can obtain the data with which to plot a second point, the entire curve may have shifted without our knowing it."[19] The value, in the case of condoms, of understanding that consumer demand is price inelastic and that there is a kinked demand curve at the producer level is in providing a theoretical framework for strategic planning. It is important to know what market tactics are apt to prove fruitful and what ones are apt to be a waste of effort. Knowing the demand configurations provides points of reference for such decisions. It is not necessary to have actual numerical demand curve data in order to comprehend the strengths and limitations of a firm's market situation."[20]

The kinked demand curve exists in the condom industry because under current circumstances it is in the best interests of the retailers, the manufacturers, and the economy. The structural arrangements which made the kinked demand configuration possible result in more efficient operation than is likely under competitive conditions. If condom manufacturers had direct access to the consumer, they could charge prices high enough to make inefficient manufacturing levels profitable and thus remove the kink in the demand curve. Direct access would dilute the retailers' power and increase their incentive to seek lower producer prices. Manufacturers' profit margins would be squeezed by a combination of higher costs based on lower volume operation, smaller market shares, increased promotional expenses to meet increased competition, and intensified price competition. The retailers' expenses would also rise because of the necessity of maintaining more skus. The price to the consumer probably would not fall because of the inelastic demand curve and increased costs being passed along by manufacturers and merchants. In short, the industry would no longer be an oligopoly. In his analysis of the kinked demand curve in oligopoly, Sylos-Labini concluded: "A new large firm attracted by the high profit rate could not achieve it (entry) and, to boot, would cause losses to all firms. The alternative to a price yielding high profits to large firms is not a price which equals cost, but sheer chaos."[21]

(This study only considers the condom industry. However, the findings raise questions concerning a more general applicability. Oligopolies mostly occur under conditions of inelastic demand; many manufacturers face oligopsonistic distribution channels; most participants in a business tend to accommodate the most efficient structure; etc. Entry-detering prices provide a rationale for a kinked demand curve [i.e., higher prices are avoided because they would invite new competitors, while lower prices are avoided because they are more apt to cut profits than to raise sales. An entry-detering price strategy is only practical in price-inelastic markets].)

The existence of such power on the part of the retailers raises the question of why they do not force out all but the most efficient producer. This theoretically could lead to lower costs and a lower price. Several reasons make this impractical:

1. With only one supplier there is no reason to assume that in the longer term any cost savings due to economies of scale would be passed on to the retailers. As a monopolist it would be possible for the manufacturer to raise prices and lower the retailer's margins.

2. The economies of scale diminish rapidly once the threshold output level is exceeded. This limits any cost advantage to a sole supplier.

3. If something happens to restrict the monopolist's output (e.g., a strike, a fire, etc.) no alternative source of supply would be available.

4. Competition encourages technical innovation[22] which, while limited in the condom industry, is still necessary.

Since its introduction in 1939, the kinked demand curve has been a subject of considerable debate among economists. In his 1978 article in *Economic Inquiry* (see footnote 7) George Stigler surveyed the literature through 1976 and found 189 references (143 favoring the kinked demand curve, 29 neutral, and 17 unfavorable). A print-out from the *Economic Literature Index* showed another 16 articles can be added to cover the period through 1988. It should be noted that, while Dr. Stigler is not an enthusiastic supporter of the kinked demand curve, he does not claim that it does not exist. He wrote "of course there are many episodes where a price increase by one firm has not been followed by others or where price decreases have been followed. The examples (articles) suggest only that no extensive careful search of supporting evidence has been made by anyone."[23]

Insights

This analysis into the competitive situation in the condom industry has provided a number of insights into the better understanding of an oligopoly as described in the following paragraphs.

First, three firms dominate the condom industry in the United States and thereby fulfill the main requirement for an oligopolistic market structure.

Until a few years ago, a case could have been made for describing condom manufacturing as a duopoly for all practical purposes. Youngs and Schmid clearly controlled the business. They narrowly focused their efforts on condoms. (Both had some other products, but these represented small portions of their respective sales volumes.) Today, Carter-Wallace, the present owner of the Youngs operation, sells a broad and diversified line of health products. Schmid, while part of LIG, has not broadened its line appreciably but has the potential for doing so. Other competitors, while comparatively small in condom sales, are starting to erode formerly unassailable market positions.

Industry structures are formed based on one set of competitive and historic circumstances and in a dynamic economy are changed by other occurrences.

Second, there are few physical differences between condoms. All the well-known analyses of oligopoly start with the assumption that the industry's products are homogeneous. This was true of Cournot's mineral springs, and it carried into the works of Edgeworth, Hotelling, and Sweezy. The important distinction that Hotelling introduced was that while the products are physically identical, they are often differentiated in the eyes of the buyers. (Hotelling used location as the basis for differentiation in his example.) Sylos-Labini postulated two types of oligopoly: "concentrated," with the products being identical; and "differentiated," where each firm's offerings had its own consumer appeal.[24] Condoms are essentially homogeneous; the main point of difference is the level of confidence with which the consumer views the product. As a result, condoms are hard to classify in Sylos-Labini's terms. The condom industry consists of a few firms with essentially uniform technology and products. Thus it meets the requirements for a concentrated oligopoly. Yet the products of each producer are considered to be different by consumers, placing it in the differentiated column.

Third, competition in the condom industry is based on consumer preferences. It is what users believe that differentiates condom brands rather than their physical characteristics. Confidence in the leading brands is the greatest factor. The consumer has a notion of what a product is worth to him or her. While each individual may not indulge in a detailed analysis in determining a preferred condom brand, a vote is cast with every purchase. The consumer decides how much it is worth to use a product whose quality is known and the peace of mind arising out of such assurance. Conscious consideration of preferences is dependent on the relative price of the product, its cost in relation to the consumer's total resources, and the performance expected. As low-priced merchandise that is purchased infrequently, condoms do not qualify for reappraisal on each transaction.

Fourth, consumer demand for condoms is price inelastic. As demonstrated by the wide variation in prices obtained by retailers, no more condoms are sold at low prices nor are any less bought at high prices. This also fits the assumptions used in studies of oligopolistic competition.

The difference shown by analyzing the condom industry is that the condom manufacturers have no way of capitalizing on this situation. Access to the consumer is controlled by the retailers.

Fifth, the condom manufacturer faces a "kinked" demand curve as described by Paul Sweezy in his article on "Demand Under Conditions of Oligopoly."[25] Price increases are not permitted by the relative strength of the distribution organizations. Conversely, competitors will not allow significant opportunities to be gained by price cuts. A contribution of this study of the condom industry is in showing how the industry price level was reached since a kinked demand curve permits little movement. When the modern condom industry started to emerge in the 1920s, the business was characterized by many small producers supplying local markets through a variety of outlets. Youngs and Schmid built their positions by offering reliable, standardized products for sale exclusively through druggists at high markups. Initially, it is reasonable to assume, both producer and retail prices were set based on the costs of manufacturing and distribution with due consideration of the prices charged by potential competitors. Over the years this level was adjusted to act as a deterrent to the entry of new competitors and became the industry standard.

Oligopoly price tends to be sticky. It changes infrequently due to significant shifts in costs which are justifiable in the eyes of the retailer. The producer price level reflects manufacturing costs and provides a fair profit at a level of output which is above a level of operation designed to discourage entry by new domestic producers. (Most health and beauty aid products manufacturers report around a 10 percent pretax return on sales revenues during an average year.) Since condom prices do not fluctuate, when demand increases, profits rise sharply in both total dollars and on a unit basis up to the level of capacity operation. When sales fall, profits drop more steeply than volume.

The established condom manufacturers enjoy monopoly profits (i.e., the amount by which price exceeds the average operating cost including an imputed return on capital) by virtue of control over the means of production with its attendant economies of scale. This only becomes possible at relatively large shares of the market. This differs from the usual circumstance where monopoly profits are associated with the control of prices but confirms the findings of Demsetz and Semmler.[26]

Sixth, list prices are not necessarily an accurate reflection of the price level. The condom industry is characterized by a large number of so-called nonprice actions that lower the costs to the retailer without changing the published prices. The effect is merely another route to reaching an industry price which would have been attained in any event. The difference is in the inefficient efforts which manufacturers expend in attempting to gain a competitive advantage.

The main benefit to a practice like a slotting allowance is to provide a barrier against smaller brands striving to gain a position with the retailer. It is ineffective against major players who can easily match or beat any competitive offer.

Seventh, nonprice competition prevails among condom manufacturers as is characteristic of an oligopoly. Most discussions of nonprice competition point to advertising as a key area for product differentiation. The usual assumption is that print and/or broadcast media are the key avenues for delivering the manufacturer's message to the consumer. However, these advertising methods are expensive and not always appropriate to small-volume items. Condoms, like other small purchase merchandise such as hair pins and curlers, combs, etc., rely most heavily on point-of-purchase displays like packaging, display ads, etc.

Chapter 6

Industry Regulation

Overview

For the last 115 years federal regulation has played an important role in the U.S. condom industry. From 1873 to 1927, the Comstock Laws kept the industry regional and fragmented. Until the mid–1970s, local statutes often gave the druggist the exclusive right to sell condoms, thus helping Youngs and Schmid capture a dominant position in condom manufacturing. The 1976 amendments to the Food, Drug, and Cosmetics Act classified condoms as a medical device subject to regulation. This provided the basis for the current regulated status of the condom industry.

The Federal Food, Drug, and Cosmetics Act of 1938 authorized the regulation of medical devices. In this act the term "device" was defined to mean "any instrument, apparatus, or contrivance, including any of its components, parts, and accessories, intended for use in the diagnosis, cure, mitigation, treatment or prevention of disease in man or other animals, or intended to effect the structure or any function of the body of man or other animals. From the legislative history, it is clear that the term device was intended to include . . . contraceptives."[1]

The 1938 act limited action by the FDA to "only when a device is deemed to be adulterated or misbranded."[2] Consequently, the FDA was to protect the public from unsafe and ineffective medical devices. It gave the FDA authority to regulate medical devices: to collect data, establish standards for the finished product, the conditions under which they are manufactured, the product claims, and required labeling. With the 1976 amendments, condom manufacture and sale came under federal scrutiny. Condoms are now classified as obstetrical and gynecological devices covered by sections 884.5300, condom, and 884.5310, condom with spermicidal lubricant.[3]

Until 1986 the regulations covered by the 1976 amendments were not stringently enforced with regard to condoms. Unfit products were not permitted to be marketed, and plants were inspected. However, since the use of condoms was not expanding rapidly and the outcomes of product failure were not considered catastrophic, the surveillance was relatively benign. With the recognition that condoms are the only known effective defense against the transmission of the AIDS virus, however, condoms became life-protecting devices. The surgeon general of the United States endorsed the use of condoms. With greater public visibility, the sale of condoms expanded rapidly. Responding to these developments, the FDA increased enforcement of condom standards, including both product and manufacturing facility inspections. This led to product recalls, improved operating procedures, more extensive contact among firms, the government, and health agencies, and ultimately higher operating costs for manufacturers. Today the condom industry is closely monitored, which is a condition that may offer another barrier to entry into this business. This section of the study describes the way the FDA regulates the condom industry and reviews the effects of this surveillance on the structure and competitive actions within the industry.

Product Specifications

Condoms are Class II Medical Devices. They are required to conform to performance standards that "provide reasonable (proof) of a device's safe and effective performance . . . a standard shall include 1) provisions respecting the construction, components, ingredients and properties of the device . . . 2) provisions for . . . testing . . . by the manufacturer . . . 3) provisions for the measurement of performance characteristics . . . 4) provisions requiring that the sale and distribution of the device be restricted. In addition, a . . . standard can require certain labeling for the proper use of a device."[4] The product specifications for condoms are contained in A.S.T.M. D 3492–83. This specification was voluntarily developed by the condom manufacturers and adopted by the FDA.

The materials section of the product specification only requires that condoms be "manufactured from good quality latex rubber conforming to specification D 1076." There is no requirement to use food-grade ingredients. Condoms are used by some persons during oral sex, which may lead to revision of this specification.

The condom design must include an "integral rim" and the dimensions of the condom are specified by type and class. Measurements can range from 150–200mm in length, 47–54mm in width, and 0.03–0.09mm in thickness. The weight of a condom can not exceed 2 grams.

The condom supplier is responsible for the performance of all inspection requirements. Physical characteristics include a minimum tensile strength of 15,000 pounds psa and elongation before breakage of 625 percent. The quality inspection requirements allow:

- 4 percent failure with respect to dimensions.

- 2.5 percent failure in tensile strength and elongation.

• 0.4 percent failure due to leakage.

All specifications are based on sample lots.

Good Manufacturing Practice

The methods used in, and the facilities and controls for, the manufacture, packing, and storage of a medical device must conform to good manufacturing practice (GMP). All procedures must be formally established and documented, and copies of these procedures submitted to the FDA for approval. The GMP provisions include:

1. Adequate organizational structure and sufficient personnel are required to assure that the formally established and implemented quality assurance programs can be performed and documented. In addition to review of the production records, the quality assurance programs and procedures also cover: all components, labeling, finished condoms and condoms manufactured, processed, packaged, and/or held under contract by another company.

2. The facilities for manufacturing, assembling, packaging, holding, testing, and labeling are to be suitable for adequate cleaning, maintenance, and other necessary operations. Space and fixtures must be adequate to prevent mix-ups and to assure the orderly handling of all raw materials, work in process, finished devices, equipment, testing operations, and quarantined products.

3. Manufacturing equipment is to be appropriate to the manufacture of condoms. Written maintenance schedules must be readily available and used for periodic documented inspections.

4. Written procedures are required for the receipt, storage, and handling of components to prevent damage, mix-up, contamination, or other adverse effects. On receipt all components are to be inspected, sampled, and tested for conformance to specifications.

5. Written manufacturing specifications and processing procedures must assure that the device conforms to specification.

6. Controls must be enforced on packaging and labeling to maintain their integrity and prevent mix-ups.

7. Written procedures are required for the warehousing and distribution of approved finished devices.

Table 6A. Condom Recalls in 1987 and Early 1988

Date of FDA Recall Report	*Distributor*	*Manufacturer*	*Number Recalled*
July 1, 8, 1987	Nat. San. Lab	Ansell	14,688
	Circle	Circle	99,360
	Schmid	Schmid	26,208
July 15, 23	Schmid	Schmid	2,830,032
July 29, Aug. 5	Circle	Circle	14,400
Aug. 26, Sept. 2	M & M	Dongkuk	170,424
Dec. 23, 30	Nat. San. Lab	Ansell	4,320
Jan. 13, 20, 1988	Mentor	Circle	11,861

These data were taken from FDA enforcement reports. No other condom recalls were reported between January 1, 1987, and January 31, 1988.

---

8. Finished device inspection requirements include: written procedures for checking on specification conformance, sampling plans based on valid statistical criteria, and quarantine or comparable controls until the finished device is released.

9. Records must be kept of the devices produced, their manufacturing history, and all complaints. These must be available for review and copying by the FDA and must be kept a minimum of two years.

Under the Medical Device Amendments of 1976, the FDA is required to inspect each condom plant at least once every two years.

The law is clear, and the FDA inspection procedures are rigorous as documented above. The regulations apply to "any condom manufactured, imported or offered for import in any state or territory of the United States, the District of Columbia, or the Commonwealth of Puerto Rico."[5]

Enforcement

The FDA's Center for Devices and Radiological Health is responsible for regulating medical devices, including condoms. In early 1987 the FDA revised its strategy for regulating condoms. With increasing promotion of condoms to protect against STDs, especially AIDS, condoms became a top priority for the FDA in 1987. The agency has strengthened its inspection of condom manufacturers and repackagers of domestic and imported condoms. The FDA also provides guidance for the labeling of condoms.

A check of the FDA enforcement reports, starting with January 1986, showed no condoms were recalled before July 1987. In March 1987 the FDA reactivated an established procedure to test for condom leakage that

Table 6B. FDA Condom Sampling Program

A. Lot Size Up to 35,000			
Type Plan	*No. Condoms to Be Examined*	*No. of Defective Condoms*	
		Accept	*Reject*
Single	Up to 315	3	4
Multiple			
1st 80	80	*	3
2nd 80	160	0	3
3rd 80	240	1	4
4th 80	320	2	5
5th 80	400	3	5
6th 80	480	4	6
7th 80	560	6	7
B. Lot Size 35,001 to 150,000			
Single	Up to 500	5	6
Multiple			
1st 125	125	*	4
2nd 125	250	1	5
3rd 125	375	2	7
4th 125	500	3	7
5th 125	625	5	8
6th 125	750	7	9
7th 125	875	9	10
C. Lot Size 150,001 to 500,000			
Single	Up to 800	7	8
Multiple			
1st 200	200	*	4
2nd 200	400	1	6
3rd 200	600	3	8
4th 200	800	5	10
5th 200	1,000	7	11
6th 200	1,200	10	12
7th 200	1,400	13	14

had not been used for over a decade. As shown on Table 6A, a significant number of condoms were recalled in July and August 1987. Since then the FDA apparently has uncovered fewer lots of condoms that were released by the manufacturers for sale and which failed to pass the FDA's sampling criteria. This requirement allows a maximum of 4 leakers (when filled with 300ml. of water) per 1000 condoms based on an approved statistical sampling procedure.

Between April and August 1987, the FDA tested over 54,000 condoms from 219 lots. These tests showed an average leakage rate of 3.3 condoms per 1000 for all lots approved. Twenty percent of the randomly chosen lots were rejected. The statistical leakage rate for the 41 lots that failed ranged from 5 to 20 per 1000. Eleven of the rejected lots were manufactured in the United States. The other 30 lots were imported condoms.

The sampling inspection plan used by the FDA is shown on Table 6B. The FDA field offices collect samples and test the products for leakage, using either a single or multiple sampling plan. For example, in a lot of up to 35,000 condoms, 576 (4 gross) condoms would be collected. (The FDA Sampling Guide requires that sample sizes consist of more condoms than the maximum number of units to be tested—e.g., 560 for lots up to 35,000 condoms.) Using the single sample plan, up to 315 condoms could be tested. If the sample contains three or fewer defective condoms, the lot is accepted. Four or more defectives and the lot would be rejected and subject to seizure.

Using the multiple sampling approach for the same lot size, up to 560 condoms would be tested in lots of 80. If less than 3 defective condoms were found in the first group, the FDA inspectors would be required to test a second batch of 80. If three or more defective condoms were found in the first 80, the entire lot would be rejected.

If by the completion of the second interval—160 condoms—no leaking condoms have been found, then the entire lot can be accepted. As long as the number of defective condoms is above the acceptance level and below the reject level, additional groups of 80 are tested. Following this pattern, if necessary, testing would continue until the maximum number of condoms for the lot size (in this example 560) have been tested. If at this point the sample contains six or fewer defective condoms, the lot is accepted. Seven or more defective devices leads to rejection.

In addition to broadening its sampling and inspection of condoms in commercial distribution, the FDA strengthened its inspection of condom manufacturers and repackagers. On inspection, most firms were required to correct some practices not in compliance with GMP requirements. The most severe deficiencies were found at the Circle Rubber plant in Newark, New Jersey. On examination of this facility and the operating practices of the firm between May 5 and 12, 1988, FDA inspectors noted "serious violations . . . and deviations from the implementing regulations" (of the Federal Food, Drug and Cosmetics Act). Ultimately this led to a shutdown of the plant in late summer–early fall of 1988. FDA representatives remained on the site while the violations were corrected.

The recalls and rigorous plant inspections have improved the protection of the public's interests and increased the costs of the condom manufacturers. As indicated in my cost estimates in Chapter 3, 36.6 percent of condom manufacturing costs are normally spent on quality assurance. Most manufacturing processes result in rejects, defective products that never leave the plant and are provided for in the cost of manufacturing. However, when the level of rejects exceeds the historically tolerable level, costs rise substantially. When the FDA more rigorously enforced compliance of condom standards, both rejects and costs increased.

Foreign producers are subject to GMP requirements as well as finished product specifications. All suppliers must submit written documentation describing their facilities and procedures. However, to date the FDA has only conducted on-site inspections of domestic plants. Compliance by foreign manufacturers is accepted based on the information they provide and inspection of final products. This situation could provide an advantage for the off-shore producer and is an example of unequal enforcement of the regulations.

Section 510(k)

When they want to introduce a new product, condom manufacturers usually file notification under section 510(k) of the Food, Drug and Cosmetics Act. This is the simplest and quickest way to introduce a medical device.

Under section 513(f) of the act, a device not commercially distributed in interstate commerce prior to May 28, 1976 (the date of enactment of the Medical Device Amendments of 1976), is automatically classified in Class III—the most rigorously regulated class—unless it is reclassified or it is substantially equivalent to one of two types of devices: a device that was in interstate commercial distribution before May 28, 1976, or a postenactment device that has been classified into Class I or II.[6] A condom avoids reclassification if it is substantially equivalent to condoms sold before May 28, 1976. The Medical Device Amendment did not specify any standard for a manufacturer's claim of substantial equivalence. Under section 510(k) the manufacturer is only required to report the class to which the device belongs and wait 90 days before introducing it into interstate commerce. However, based on the stated purpose of the Medical Device Amendment, the FDA requires that two devices must serve the same purpose, and their performance must be equivalent in safety and effectiveness. The devices need not be identical. Therefore, even under the simplified procedures of section 510(k), the FDA often requires clinical data supporting the claim of substantial equivalence.

Foreign manufacturers also use 510(k) filings to get their condoms approved for sale in the United States. In 1987, when some condom suppliers were anxious to obtain condoms to sell under their brands, they helped off-shore producers through the maze of regulatory requirements. This action essentially neutralized a potential obstacle to foreign entry into the U.S. condom market.

Traceability

Records are an essential feature of the FDA's regulatory process. The Medical Device Amendments require that it be possible to trace a device through the various channels of distribution. Individual or batch numbers or codes are used to facilitate the recovery of products found to be defective. They also provide a means of determining the history of a particular lot of condoms to ascertain the source of the product failure. Every lot of condoms must leave a paper trail which can be easily followed back to the starting materials.

Labeling

The package used for condoms, like the packages for most other medical devices, must be clearly labeled with: (1) the name and place of business of the manufacturer, packer, or distributor; and (2) clear and adequate directions for use. False or misleading representations on a label makes the product "misbranded" and subject to seizure. Care must be taken not to use words which make or imply claims that are not backed by clinical evidence that has been accepted by the FDA. The FDA is very particular about such wording. For example, in spite of a wealth of evidence, it was only on April 7, 1987, that condom manufacturers were given permission to claim that condoms provided barrier protection against AIDS without submitting a separate 510(k) premarket notification along with clinical proof. Even then, the words were carefully chosen and phrased: "When used properly, the latex condom may prevent the transmission of many sexually transmitted diseases (STDs) such as syphilis, gonorrhea, chlamydial infections, genital herpes and AIDS. It cannot eliminate the risk. For maximum protection it is important to follow the accompanying instructions. Failure to do so may result in loss of protection. During intimate contact lesions and various body fluids can transmit STDs. Therefore, the condom should be applied before contact."[7] (After reading such a statement, one wonders whom the FDA is protecting. Most studies indicate that the script on condom packages is seldom, if ever, read.) The FDA statement was for use by all condom suppliers. If a manufacturer wished to make a claim differentiating his product such as "specifically designed for AIDS," "better than other condoms," etc., a 510(k) would be required along with convincing clinical evidence before the FDA would consider allowing it to be used.

The Surgeon General

While federal regulation may have raised the costs of condom manufacturers, few can deny that it was the surgeon general of the United States's *Report on AIDS* that boosted the industry to its present level of demand. When Surgeon General Koop's *Report on Acquired Immunodeficiency Syndrome* was published in October 1986, it not only endorsed the use of condoms as the only known sexual protection against the transmission of AIDS, other than abstinence, it also dramatically documented the horror of AIDS.

AIDS is caused by a virus that invades the blood stream. There are no physically apparent symptoms of the illness. There is no known cure. AIDS can infect anyone, white or black, male or female, heterosexual, homosexual, or bisexual. Men who have sexual relations with other men are considered especially at risk. According to the surgeon general's report, about 70 percent of the AIDS victims throughout the country are male homosexuals and bisexuals. "Infections results from a sexual relationship with an infected person." The risk of infection increases according to the number of sexual partners. The more partners, the greater the risk of AIDS infection.

In recommending personal safety measures, the report specifically mentions "using a rubber [condom] during [start to finish] sexual intercourse [vaginally or rectally]."

The impact this report had on the media provided a surge in free (and perhaps more credible) advertising. With constant reminders of the terrors of AIDS came the 50 percent increase in condom sales in 1987. Since the surgeon general and those who report the news have become less vociferous, the growth in the use of condoms has eased.

Economic Analysis of Regulation

In his book *The Structure of American Industry*[8] Walter Adams wrote: "Ideally, competition and regulation are opposite sides of the same coin. In theory, both are directed at the same objectives: efficient use of resources and protection against exploitation. . . . Regulation as originally conceived, was to be both a supplement to and substitute for competition . . . the visible hand of public regulation was to replace the invisible hand mentioned by Adam Smith, in order to protect consumers against extortionate charges, restriction of output, deterioration of services and unfair discrimination. This was the rationale of the Interstate Commerce Act of 1887."[9] In *Innovation in the Pharmaceutical Industry* David Schwartzman noted: "the field of industrial organization, within which the investigation of the drug industry has fallen, has been devoted to the study of the economics of competition and monopoly. . . . The drug industry is simply one of many industries. That some issues may be peculiar to it is not noticed nor that some of these issues may be more important for public policy."[10] Thus, Schwartzman argued for the consideration of the impact of regulatory actions on an industry-by-industry basis so as not to overlook important unique features of each business.

Pharmaceuticals like condoms are regulated by the FDA and must comply with many of the same rules. Therefore, I made a brief, but probably representative, sampling of economic studies of regulation of the drug industry. My purpose was to determine if there might be significance in these studies for condoms. Unfortunately, most focused on issues which do not effect condoms: monopoly (see reference 10)—the condom industry is too small and has too little impact on consumer expenditures to attract antitrust attention; competition (see footnotes 10 and 11)—both the drug and condom industries try to avoid price competition but there are more real, as opposed to perceived, differences among drugs than there are among condoms; research and development (see footnotes 10 and 11)—pharmaceutical firms perform extensive research and derive most of their monopoly power from the patents resulting from such activity, while research on condoms has been minimal and to date no firm has gained a significant competitive advantage through product innovation (Mentor Corp. is an example of a firm that tried).

Regulation of the condom industry has developed in line with the desire to protect the public from fraudulent or unsafe medical devices (for further study see footnotes 12 and 13). R.S. McCutcheon described the growth of federal regulation as follows: "Federal regulation is quite extensive, but it is quite piecemeal . . . law is more or less like Topsey: it just grows. It grows in response to need, usually long overdue; it grows in response to special interests that we would usually be better off without; and it is often made with too little attention to the facts as they really are and the effects of the law after passage. When a regulatory law is passed, it always gives birth immediately to one or more governmental bureaus or adds new parts to bureaus already in existence. After formation of a bureau, we get a new set of laws as an outgrowth of the parent act as a result of promulgation, by rule making, by practice, by interpretation, and by administrative decision to settle questions growing from the new regulation. Thus, we get regulatory law not only by legislation, but also by bureaucratic fiat."[14] Table 6C lists consumer safety laws and regulations mentioned in McCutcheon's article. My purpose is to illustrate that the economic effects of regulation are felt by many industries.

The condom industry provides an uncomplicated example of how government regulation can effect an industry's products, costs, marketing practices, and organizational structure. The FDA condom regulations define the dimensions of the product, its components, ingredients, and properties. The methods and extent of testing are clearly delineated as well as the final specifications. The requirements of "good manufacturing practice" place limits on the plant facilities and techniques. Once these parameters have been set, the manufacturing cost of the product has for the most part been fixed.

The packaging requirements are also closely defined. These include: the materials of package construction, wording on the package, storage and shipping instructions, and shelf life. In effect the packaging and distribution costs are closely circumscribed.

Once all costs are fixed, a floor on the price is clearly established.

When the "little Comstock laws" were in effect, government agencies

Table 6C. Outline of Consumer Safety Laws and Regulations and Enforcing Agencies

Agencies

1. Health Education and Welfare (HEW)
   A. Food and Drug Administration (FDA)
      1. Regulates food, drugs, cosmetics, and medical devices
      2. Determines safety of new drugs
      3. Provides standards of identity, quality and fill of containers
      4. Provides for periodic factory inspection
      5. Sets standards for food coloring
      6. Controls food additives
      7. Controls labeling of food products
      8. Requires that drugs be shown to be effective
      9. National Drug Code Directory
      10. Regulation of radiation from consumer products, electronic production radiation, radiation in the healing arts, occupational exposure to radiation, research, and technical assistance relating to these
   B. Bureau of Community Environmental Management
   C. Bureau of Occupational Safety and Health
   D. National Institute of Occupational Safety and Health
      1. Provides for research
      2. Provides for regulations relating to exposure, medical examination, and tests of workers
   E. Drug abuse law as it relates to medical research and educational aspects. Recommendations to the Attorney General for listing controlled substances after scientific and medical evaluation
   F. Federal Hazardous Substances Act
      a. Defines hazardous substances
      b. Defines toxic, corrosive, irritant, and similar terms
      c. Regulates toys and substances used by children
      d. Provides for banning of hazardous substances
   G. Child Protection and Toy Safety Act of 1969
      a. Specifies more clearly the prohibited hazards
      b. Gives the Secretary, HEW, power to act
   H. The Poison Prevention Packaging Act of 1970
      a. Improved bottle closures for prevention of child opening
      b. Provides for standards for packaging of certain household substances
   I. Public Health Cigarette Smoking Act of 1967
      a. Provides for warning on cigarette package
   J. Fair Packaging and Labeling Act
   K. Federal Caustic Poison Act
   L. Flammable Fabrics Act
   M. Prohibition Against Future Use of Lead-Based Paint
2. The Department of Agriculture
      a. Now mostly advisory in relation to the use of pesticides
3. Department of Transportation
      a. Regulates shipment of dangerous materials
      b. Regulates labeling and proximity of shipments
4. Department of Interior
      a. Internal control of a wide use of pesticides and similar agents

Table 6C. Outline of Consumer Safety Laws and Regulations and Enforcing Agencies (cont.)

Agencies

- b. Has control of studies and regulation of ocean pollution and similar problems through its agency, NOAA

5. Federal Trade Commission
   - a. Controls labeling and promotion of toxic substances
6. Department of Justice
   - a. Bureau of Narcotics and Dangerous Drugs (BNDD)
     1. Rehabilitation
     2. Control and enforcement
     3. Importation and exportation and revenue laws
7. Environmental Protection Agency (EPA)
   - a. Controls licensing, distribution, and tolerance limits of pesticides
   - b. Air pollution
   - c. Water pollution
   - d. Solid waste management
   - e. Radiologic health (with some exceptions)
   - f. Environmental quality as related to ecologic systems

Agencies

   - g. Radiation protection standards
   - h. The Clean Air Act
   - i. National Emission Standards Act
   - j. Noise Pollution and Abatement Act
8. Atomic Energy Commission (AEC)
   - a. Sets strict radioactive packaging requirements and requires shipper responsibility
9. Federal Aviation Agency (FAA)
   - a. Licenses pesticide applications from aircraft
10. Department of Labor
    - a. Occupational Safety and Health Act Enforces rules for industrial safety
11. White House
    - a. Special Action Office on Drug Abuse Prevention
    - b. The Council for Environmental Quality

---

defined who could sell condoms: druggists. These laws established the retail marketing channels and also defined the ways the product could be promoted (no advertising). In this way the evolution of the industry as an oligopoly was fostered. While these laws are no longer in force, the effects on consumer behavior still linger. Habits change slowly. The industry structure and trade practices established decades ago continue to dominate the industry.

There are few examples, other than direct government ownership and operation, where an industry is so closely controlled. It is apparent that this situation was not preplanned; as McCutcheon says, it just grew like

Topsey (see footnote 14). As is often the case,[15] the FDA solicited the industry's cooperation in establishing the condom specifications and until 1987[16,17] enforcement was not especially rigorous.

The close regulation of the condom industry also serves to make it more difficult for firms to enter the business. Dr. Schwartzman's remarks on research in the pharmaceutical industry can be generalized to cover condoms as well. Schwartzman says that "Increased demands by the FDA for evidence of efficacy and safety . . . have reduced the number of innovations."[18] A lack of new products is generally symptomatic of a stagnant business.

But the economic implications of FDA regulation of the condom industry are counterbalanced by substantial social welfare benefits. As J. Richard Crout, director of the Bureau of Drugs, Food and Drug Administration, said, as quoted by Oswald Brownlee "I would emphasize strongly . . . that the Food and Drug Administration regulates health policy, not economic matters. That is terribly important to understand. We do not pay any attention to the economic consequences of our decisions, and the law does not ask us to. That does not mean that FDA people are necessarily lacking in breadth as people or that we are blind to costs, but the point I emphasize strongly is that our decisions deal solely with safety and effectiveness."[19] The FDA clearly recognizes that its regulations will affect industry costs. It is unfortunate that the financial benefits of these actions are difficult to quantify. How do we calculate the cost of something that might have occurred if these regulations were not enforced? (Some insights might be apparent in Chapter 8 which discusses the costs to society of the nonuse of condoms.) Another positive aspect of condom regulation is the benefit to manufacturers based on the consumer confidence in the products generated by the knowledge that strict controls are enforced.

The government actions which led to the formation of an oligopolistic structure may well have resulted in the most practical and efficient organization of this industry. Returning to the quotation from Adams cited at the start of this section, it seems a case could be made for supporting the opinion that the regulation of the condom industry provides "efficient use of resources and protection."

Insights

Governmental regulation has played a role in the condom industry for at least 115 years (I did not investigate the period before 1873). The economic significance of this regulation has varied with specific laws and the level of enforcement as indicated by the following.

First, before 1927, the Comstock Laws provided a barrier to the formation of an efficient condom industry. The Comstock Laws kept the condom industry local and many of its activities hidden.

When the intent of the laws was modified through court proceedings to define a legal use for condoms and prescribe a single channel of distribution—drugstores—the law worked toward the establishment of an oligopoly by providing an important barrier to new entrants.

Second, most economic discussions of the role of government focus on three roles: the production of public goods and services, transfer payments, and taxation. Studies of the role of government regulation is usually restricted to antitrust actions or interstate commerce. However, the actions of the FDA relative to condoms directly effect the product, the manufacturing cost, and the methods of competition. By setting and enforcing tight specifications on the condom industry, the FDA has made the products and their level of quality homogeneous. The cost of manufacturing is raised by the requirements for "good manufacturing practice," more stringent quality standards, a higher level of testing, and increased staff to fulfill government reporting and liaison requirements. By controlling product claims, the FDA restricts the flexibility of manufacturers in attempting to differentiate their brands. By defining the cost parameters government regulations establish a pricing floor.

Manufacturers view the financial effects of these actions as taxes which raise their costs and restrict their ability to increase profits in the face of an inflexible industry price level. A welfare economist sees the FDA's role as adding value to the consumer by improving the reliability of the product and the public's confidence in the merchandise. Cost additions caused by regulation are offset by benefits to society.

Another effect is to further level any cost differential among manufacturers since at least one-third of the manufacturing cost is directly related to quality assurance. With tighter controls producers have less opportunity to uncover manufacturing savings other than those related to the level of output.

Third, the close control of the condom industry is a barrier to entry by firms not familiar with operating in a government-regulated environment. However, it also acts to provide a potential advantage to overseas manufacturers. Imported condoms must comply with the finished product specifications and their manufacturers must furnish written documentation of their compliance with GMP regulations. But, unfortunately, the FDA does not inspect foreign plants and their authority, if they did inspect, is questionable. All the FDA could do is restrict the importing of a manufacturer's goods into the United States. They could not force the shutdown of plants as they have done in the U.S. In addition freedom from inspection lowers costs on liaison activities.

Fourth, the product recalls in 1987 serve to illustrate a problem which has affected the competitiveness of other U.S. manufactured products. The specifications that the FDA tested condoms against were recognized requirements long before 1987. The manufacturers knew they were expected to comply, and the public had a right to feel they could trust in this compliance. Yet, either intentionally or through neglect they were selling inferior products. The attitude seems to have been that, since no one complained before, the products were "good enough." This frame of mind has led to the decline of U.S. competitiveness in several other industries where America used to set world standards. It may well be that the FDA did the condom manufacturers a favor by reminding them that they were in a business where consumers are entitled to assurance that they are receiving a quality product. In the past, in such industries as automobiles, consumer electronics, etc., American manufacturers lost major market shares before awakening to the fact that they were no longer producing the caliber of goods that was the basis for the firm's past success. Hopefully U.S. condom manufacturers have learned their lessons sufficiently to prevent loss of this business due to insufficient quality or product development.

Chapter 7

Consumer Acceptance

Overview

The acceptance, sale, and usage of condoms in the United States is based on a variety of factors:

1. The number of males and females in each age bracket of the population

2. The influence of immigration on the size and composition of each age group

3. The frequency with which members of each age group engage in sexual intercourse

4. The type of sexual intercourse: vaginal, rectal, or oral

5. Individual preferences for sexual partners: heterosexual, homosexual, or bisexual

6. The choice of contraceptives: none, pill, condom, etc.

7. The fear of transmission of STDs and the resolve of individuals to protect themselves and their partners

Not only is the total U.S. population changing, but the swings between baby booms and busts cause variations in the numbers of persons in each age group. Thus, the numbers of persons in each of the age groups holding the most sexually active members change, affecting the total potential market for condoms. Sociological shifts in the sexual proclivities of members of each grouping also affect the demand for condoms. Greater sexual activity, multiple sex partners, gender choices, fears of infection, etc.—all contribute to determining the number of possible condom users.

A distinction must be made between possible and potential condom users. Not all sexually active persons use contraceptives. For example, individuals engaged in long-term monogamous relationships do not fear STD infections and may need only contraception, not barrier protection. There

Table 7A. Worldwide Use of Condoms: Percent of currently married females of childbearing ages (either 15–44 or 15–49) reporting current use of condoms

Country	*Year*	*% Using Condoms*
Japan	1979	51%
Finland	1977	32%
Denmark	1975	25%
Singapore	?	22%
United Kingdom	1976	18%
Norway	1977–78	16%
Poland	1977	14%
Italy	1979	13%
United States	1982–83	10%
Switzerland	1980	8%
Belgium (Flemish area only)	1975–76	7%
Netherlands	1982	7%
Portugal	1979–80	6%
France	1977–78	6%
Spain	1977	5%
Romania	1978	3%
Bulgaria	1976	2%
Yugoslavia	1976	2%

Source: Howard J. Goldberg, "Worldwide Use of Condoms" (Paper presented at the Conference on Condoms in the Prevention of Sexually Transmitted Diseases, Atlanta, Ga. 20 February, 1987).

---

are a number of contraceptives available in the United States, each presenting a mix of positive and negative qualities. Condom brands compete with these products as well with each other. While anyone may theoretically use condoms, the likelihood of this use materializing must be assessed in establishing the potential market.

The availability of contraceptive alternatives has a substantial impact on the market for condoms. As an example, Table 7A lists the worldwide use of condoms in a number of developed countries. While not based on recently collected information, the data in Table 7A show that Americans use condoms less than people in many other developed nations. One of the main reasons for this difference is that in many countries other contraceptive methods have either been unavailable or are unacceptable. For example, the pill is not legal for contraception in Japan, voluntary sterilization is restricted, and Japanese women are reluctant to use methods that require them to touch their own genitals. As a result, condoms are the leading contraceptive method. Japan uses about one-quarter of the world's condoms.[1] The existence of alternatives is the key factor limiting the size of the U.S. condom market. To use William Shepherd's words, "To economists the core

Table 7B. U.S. Population Projections 1983, 1988, 1993 (in Millions of People)

1983		*1988*		*1993*	
		Aver. Annual		*Aver. Annual*	
Age Group	*Mil.*	*Mil.*	*Chg. from '83*	*Mil.*	*Chg. from '88*
15–19	19.2	17.9	−1.5%	16.3	−2.0%
20–24	21.9	19.3	−2.5%	18.1	−1.5%
25–29	21.2	22.1	0.8%	19.6	−2.5%
30–34	19.1	21.3	2.2%	22.3	+0.9%
35–39	16.3	19.1	+3.3%	21.4	+2.3%
40–44	13.2	16.2	+4.2%	19.1	+1.7%
15–44	110.9	115.9	+0.9%	116.8	+0.8%

Source: Gregory Spencer, *Projections of the Population of the United States by Age, Sex, and Race 1983 to 2080,* Series P25 No. 292 (Washington, D.C.: Bureau of the Census, May 1984).

---

idea of competition is that consumers have a high degree of choice."[2] Thus while other contraceptive methods do not offer protection from the transmission of diseases, consumers have a variety of options relative to birth control.

This chapter explores the size of the potential market, the reasons for consumers' preferences, and the outlook for expanding condom usage in the United States. The objectives are to estimate the potential market size and evaluate the strategic issues that are uncovered in this investigation.

Population Shifts

Most studies of sexual activity[3] use the age range of 15–44 years as representative of the most sexually active portion of the population. The same convention is used in this book. This portion of my report investigates the implications of shifts within subsections of the 15–44 age group.

Projections by the Bureau of the Census[4] show that while the total number of persons between the ages of 15 and 44 grew less than 1 percent per year between 1983 and 1988, those in the 15–24 group declined an average of 2 percent per year (−1.5 percent for 15–19 and −2.5 percent for 20–24). Looking ahead, the number of 15–24 year olds is projected to drop another 1.5 percent per year through 1993, and the 25–29 year olds will decline an average of 2.5 percent per year. Overall, the population in the 15–44 age group is expected to average an 0.8 percent increase with an expanding percentage over 30 years of age (i.e., 43.8 percent in 1983, 48.8 percent in 1988, and 56.6 percent in 1993). The U.S. population is growing older, with the largest gains within the sexually active segment being the 35–39 year olds. (These data are listed on Table 7B.)

Table 7C. Percentage of U.S. Women Exposed to the Risk of Unwanted Pregnancies in 1987

Age Group	*15–44*	*15–17*		*18–44*	
Marital status			*Tot.*	*Marr.*	*Unwed*
Exposed	72%	39%	74%	78%	69%
Not Exposed	28%	61%	26%	22%	31%
Never had Sex	11%	55%	7%	0	15%
Infrequent Sex	4%	3%	4%	1%	9%
Hysterectomized/Menopausal	5%	0	6%	8%	2%
Infertile	2%	*	3%	2%	4%
Pregnant or Seeking Pregnancy	6%	2%	7%	11%	1%
Total	100%	100%	100%	100%	100%

Source: J.D. Forrest and R.R. Fordyce, "U.S. Women's Contraceptive Attitudes and Practice: How Have They Changed in the 1980s?," *Family Planning Perspectives* (May-June, 1988), 115. Reprinted by permission. Copyright The Allan Gutmacher Institute.

In addition to the overall aging of the population, studies show that women are having children at a later age. The U.S. Department of Health reports that "during the period from 1975 to 1984, the birth rate for women in their early thirties rose 27%, and the rate for women aged 35–39 increased 17%. Simultaneously, the birth rate for teenagers 15–19 dropped 8%, and the rate for women 20–24 fell 5%."[5] This suggests that contraceptive usage probably decreases among those in the 30–44 age group since a larger portion are seeking to become pregnant. As a consequence, any estimate of condom sales to this group should be adjusted accordingly.

The Bureau of the Census included a net immigration of 450,000 persons a year in their "middle net" projections.[6] The origins of these new citizens will have an impact on the demand for condoms. This will be influenced by the immigrants' experiences and preferences in their former homeland and their religious convictions. Unfortunately, no references dealing statistically with this topic are available. Most of the relevant data on immigrants have focused on the AIDS epidemic and will be touched upon qualitatively relative to the need for condoms.

In adjusting the population statistics to determine the size of the available market for condoms, persons who are not sexually active must be eliminated from consideration. A 1987 study[7] found that 28 percent of all women within the 15–44 age bracket were not exposed to unwanted pregnancy. The largest portion of these were 15–17 year olds who never had sex. (Details are listed on Table 7C.) Using the data on Table 7C we can calculate a rough estimate of the possible market. Since sexual intercourse normally involves two individuals and only one condom is used, it is safe to set the maximum number of users at half the population, or 58 million in 1988. Subtracting 28 percent nonparticipants yields 42 million. But not all contraceptors use condoms. The 1987 Forrest and Fordyce study (see footnote 7) also indicated that only 12 percent of all women (and men by inference) used condoms. This suggests a 1988 market of seven million couples. In order to test the reasonableness of this approach, the population numbers can be used to estimate the 1988 demand for condoms and this value then compared to the estimates of the number of condoms sold during this period (Chapters 3 and 5 present estimates for numbers sold). Using an average usage of 50–75 condoms per user per year—a figure developed as part of a Population Report study in 1982[8]—seven million users would account for 350–525 million condoms or 2.4–3.6 million gross. The retail dollar sales reported in Chapter 5 were based on 3.3 million gross, and the total retail demand presented on Table 4A was three million gross. (The greatest source of error in this test is the estimate of average condom usage.) Therefore, the available evidence seems to support the reasonableness of this approach for estimating total demand. (It is interesting to note that a decline of sexual activity with age would seem plausible. However, the few private studies that deal with this issue show little variance in the claimed frequency of sex among persons in the 15–44 age bracket. The average is around three times a week.)

This analysis of population shifts indicates a slow growth in the demand for contraceptive products through 1993. The possible number of couples who might use condoms in 1993 could be as high as 33 million, including:

- 13 million couples now relying on the pill.
- 7 million condom users.
- 5 million now using some other form of contraception.
- 8 million unprotected individuals.

Extension of the current rate of condom usage would place condom demand at 3.3–3.6 million gross for the 15–44 age group, plus, judging from the 1988 calculations, another 10 percent for persons outside this age bracket. This makes the total 3.6–4.0 million gross. The challenges for the condom manufacturers are to capture the demand represented by the eight million couples considered to be at high risk and to convert some of the 18 million using forms of contraception other than condoms.

Much of the available information on condom usage, sexual activities, etc., is "soft" data based on opinion samplings. Often the values do not cross-check. For example, assuming an average of three acts of sexual intercourse a week for the 20 percent of males claiming to be condom users, and assuming they used condoms 75 percent of the time, equates to 9.3 million gross of condoms a year ($57 \times 0.2 \times 156 \times 0.75$)—clearly an unsupportable value.

I do not wish to disparage serious surveys but rather to stress the need for selectivity as to how numbers are applied. The values used in this study are not accurate, but they provide a reasonable basis for realistic estimates. The estimated seven million condom users assumed in this study may be high or low. However, if a different size group were chosen, the average usage would need to be adjusted, since around 3.3 million gross of condoms were sold at retail in 1988. Fine tuning such estimates has significance for marketing strategies of individual firms but not for the purposes of this study. (It is important for a marketer to know if he needs to appeal to seven million customers buying 65 condoms a year or 9.3 million persons buying 49 condoms a year. It may require a different strategy to reach different numbers of potential customers.)

As a subject for economic inquiry, imperfect information is most often viewed from the perspectives of consumers' knowledge of the product and price, as illustrated by Asher Wolinsky's work[9] or manufacturers' cognizance of the activities of competitors as covered by most textbooks like Shepherd's.[10] However, information at the producer level regarding the true potential demand for the product is also imperfect. When the product has a personal use, like condoms, it becomes especially difficult to obtain reliable information. Corporations spend large sums to track consumer and competitive activity. Even the reports of sophisticated market researchers tracking seemingly simple statistics like sales by product are often far from accurate. Many books have been written on how to collect competitive intelligence (*Business Competitor Intelligence*[11] is one example); they discuss the importance and techniques of obtaining information but fail to emphasize the unavoidable incompleteness of the data. Decisions rely on estimates of past and current operations as well as forecasts of the future. The analytical techniques and formulations developed to evaluate such actions are far more reliable than most of the input data. The only practical approach is to collect information from as many sources as possible, cross-check it, use the best techniques and analytical software available, apply as much sound judgment as possible, and hope you are not too far wrong.

Attitudes Toward Sex

Between 1982 and 1987, the percentage of single women having sex increased from 68 to 76 percent. Of 57 million women in the U.S. aged 15–44, nearly 49 million (86 percent) were having sex, including 32 million married women and 17 million who were unmarried.[12] This represents a 28 percent faster growth than could be expected from the population increase in this age bracket.

Of special interest are younger persons. Their choices of contraceptives have either not yet been made or not yet fixed into habits. Most young adults lose their virginity around the age of 16 or 17. Janet Lever, in an article for *Playboy* on sex among college students,[13] reported "fear of pregnancy . . . governs their sexual choices. Unmarried, their education at stake and wanting to avoid the trauma and expense of abortion, many college women opt for the pill because they believe it provides safer contraception. . . . AIDS seems to have had little impact on the sexual behavior of straight men and women. . . . Surveys show that high school teens and collegians continue to have multiple partners because they just don't believe that STDs will strike them." Even in San Francisco, a city with high awareness of AIDS, during a time when AIDS prevention education was intensified, a University of California study found only 2 percent of the sexually active teenage girls and 8 percent of the boys used condoms every time they had intercourse.[14]

Widespread use of the pill has decreased the fear of pregnancy. The discovery of penicillin and other antibiotics that control some sexually transmitted diseases, including syphilis and gonorrhea, removed another impediment to sexual adventurousness. Traditional family and religious values have weakened. The social acceptability of out-of-wedlock childbearing and the highest divorce rate in U.S. history combined to produce a generation of one-parent families and less parental supervision. The increase in homosexual activity is evident from the gay rights movement and establishments which cater to this group. Thus, we have the sexual revolution, a sociological attitude shift which even the terror of AIDS has not been able to dampen substantially. Part of the reason for this attitude can be ascribed to the fact that far fewer heterosexual men in the United States have AIDS than homosexual or bisexual men.[15] Also, it usually takes a long time before any evidence of AIDS infection becomes apparent.

Until more people accept their personal risk in becoming infected with STDs, including AIDS, and decide to take protective action, the demand for condoms is not likely to grow much faster than the at-risk population. The basic problem is attitudinal. The level of knowledge of STDs and AIDS is high, approaching 80–86 percent. Therefore, providing more facts is unlikely to change consumer behavior relative to the use of protective condoms.

Attitudes Toward Contraception

Consumer attitudes toward contraception vary among individuals. A person's age, marital status, personal experiences, etc., impact the decision to use contraceptives and the choice of method. The 1987 Forrest and Fordyce study (see footnote 3) found, "Among women in general, at least 57 percent gave favorable ratings to four methods—oral contraceptives, condoms, vasectomy and female sterilization. No other method was favored by more than 34 percent of the women in either marital-status group. The overwhelming majority of users (more than three-quarters in each category) rated their own method as satisfactory." The message is plain: unless there is another unfavorable medical report concerning the efficacy or safety of one or more of the methods, it would be very difficult to convert individuals using sterilization or the pill to condom users.

Condom use has increased in both numbers and as a percentage of contraceptors. The 1987 study[16] showed an increase to 16 percent, up from 12 percent in 1982. (While the data were based on a survey of women, it is reasonable to generalize for the population. The condom must be worn by a male, and it normally takes a member of each sex for intercourse.)

Information contained in a private study done for Schmid Laboratories Inc. and shared with the public indicated that in October 1987 "condom usage appears to have stabilized at between one-fifth and one-quarter of all men . . . [the study showed] some weakening in the incidence of condom usage by males using any form of contraception." The Schmid press release also said that decreased condom use results from people becoming less concerned about contracting AIDS. The less frequent use of condoms came in spite of an increased perception of the effectiveness of condoms in preventing transmission of the AIDS virus. The percentage of respondents who indicated they believe condoms were "very effective" or "somewhat effective" against AIDS was 79 percent of the men and 77 percent of the women.[17]

The most common reasons given for not using a condom are:

1. Insensitivity (the barrier inhibits the sense of feel for both partners).

2. Inconvenience (condoms need to be kept handy, put on during lovemaking, and disposed of).

3. Embarrassment (the interruption of lovemaking causes unsettling moments).

4. Poor image (condoms have long been associated with adolescent escapades and venereal disease).

The first two objections are the most widely held and have received considerable attention from condom manufacturers and birth control advocates.

The Japanese have been leaders in developing new shapes and textures for condoms which have been copied by U.S. manufacturers. When Japanese manufacturers introduced ultrathin condoms designed for greater sensitivity, their sales in Japan jumped 43 percent in one year.[18]

Ways of overcoming the problems associated with interrupting the romance of the moment to put on a condom are also being researched. The favored approach is to make the act a shared experience and part of the foreplay. Studies show that 95 percent of the time the male is left with the job of putting on his own condom. However, both men and women enjoyed the experience when the woman helped mount the condom. Not only is such activity credited with overcoming the disruption problems, it also provides the woman with greater confidence. She has a chance to inspect her partner for signs of sexually transmitted disease and to make certain the condom is securely in place.

Psychologically there is a vast barrier to pass. Simply stated, many men do not like condoms. Therefore, they either do not use condoms at anytime or avoid their use whenever they feel safe. Psychologists also report that women sometimes have urges to become pregnant and consciously or unconsciously neglect to use or urge their partners to use contraceptives.

A major factor in the birth control rate—regardless of the contraceptive method—is the degree of comfort individuals have with their chosen method of birth control. The challenge is to determine how to make people comfortable with using condoms.

Homosexual Needs

Sexual practice among many homosexuals has changed as a reaction to the AIDS epidemic. For gay men there is a new emphasis on the total homosexual experience, focusing less on genital sex. Gays report an increase in selectivity of sex partners, with more interest in longer term relationships, including romance and coupling.

Gays have led the use of condoms for STD prevention. In 1985 a sample of New York City male homosexuals reported a significant increase in condom use for both insertive and receptive anal intercourse after the respondents became aware of AIDS. Prior to learning of AIDS, the men used condoms 1 percent of the time when engaging in insertive anal intercourse. The next year, 20 percent of the respondents claimed consistent condom use.[19] In 1984 39 percent of the men in a San Francisco study[20] reported having anal intercourse; 26 percent of these homosexuals used condoms. In April 1987 19 percent of respondents from San Francisco reported anal intercourse; 79 percent used condoms.

A report from the University of Amsterdam[21] stated that "Anogenital intercourse is the main risk factor for transmission of the human immunodeficiency virus in homosexual men." The high incidence of transmission of HIV infection during anal intercourse has been attributed to mucosal tears. In the Dutch tests, the overall acceptability of condoms by gays was found to be low. Condoms were considered unattractive by 68 percent of the insertive partners and 55 percent of the receptive partners. Lubricants on the condom were not liked. All participants in this study preferred "condoms of neutral appearance which affected the natural situation as little as possible."

A 1987 Denver, Colorado, study of gay men who were infected with gonorrhea or syphilis provided the following insights: the men had a high level of awareness of AIDS and STDs; the participants knew the person who was the source of their own infection; among the reasons given for not using condoms were: 72 percent lost control (because of drink, drugs, or the excitement of the moment), and 20 percent had a mistaken belief about AIDS.[22]

However, there have been notable signs of changes in sexual behavior, as shown by another Denver study by N. Judson.[23] In tracking the number of cases of gonorrhea, syphilis, and hepatitis between 1982 and 1987, with data classified among gay men, heterosexual men, and heterosexual women, all incidences declined. The change among gay men was most dramatic; their incidence of gonorrhea dropped over 90 percent. Because of the high incidence, short incubation time, easy detection, and quick cures, gonorrhea is considered to be the most accurate indicator of changes in sexual behavior.

Oral sex is another activity for which medical authorities recommend the use of condoms. In one study[24] only 10 percent of the respondents reported that they "always" use condoms for oral sex. Gays reject condoms for oral sex because of the taste and smell of the latex and/or the lubricant.

Overall, homosexual men do not like condoms any more than heterosexual men. However, because AIDS has infected more people they know, fear has lead to higher condom usage (50–90 percent) among gays than the general population.

Some observers believe that homosexual males could account for most of the increase in condom demand in 1987. Now that a large percentage of the gay community is using condoms demand is leveling off.

Effectiveness and Acceptability of Condoms

Condoms are a highly effective method of contraception and STD protection when used consistently. They require no medical supervision and are readily available. The number of accidental pregnancies among more mature, consistent condom users is low. There are no data indicating how often condoms actually break in use. With strict quality specifications and compliance monitoring, breakage is considered relatively rare when the condom is properly applied (before intercourse and completely unrolled onto an erect penis). Most failures have been traced to improper handling or use.

Use effectiveness is related to a number of personal characteristics which influence how consistently a couple uses condoms. These include age, motivation to control births or prevent infection, proper application, and the emotional state at the time of application. (Condoms are often either not used properly or improperly applied during the heat of passion or under the influence of alcohol or drugs.)

The effectiveness of condoms is increased when a spermicide is used along with the condom.

Persons who feel they have no reason to suspect an infection of AIDS or other STDs and who use condoms for contraception have shown a relatively high rate of discontinued use. Some stop because they do not like using condoms. Others deliberately use condoms only for short periods of time: before marriage, between pregnancies, or before switching to a contraceptive method with which they feel more comfortable.

The condom has historically had a bad image. Condoms are seen as inhibitors of sensitivity, troublesome to use, and not quite respectable.

But other than abstinence, the condom is the only effective protection against sexually transmitted diseases, including AIDS. The condom should be the contraceptive of choice for anyone with any risk of exposure to STDs. Unfortunately, perception, not fact, governs most retail purchases. This works in favor of the condom manufacturers when consumers choose their brands over an equivalent product. It hinders increased sales when perceptions of deficiencies are retained long after any problems have been solved.

Immigration

Immigration patterns are of interest in the analysis of the condom industry because of their impact on the transmission of the AIDS virus. Some researchers have drawn similarities between the introduction of commercial aviation and the spread of AIDS to the opening of naval trade routes and the spread of syphilis in the 15th and 16th centuries. They have also pointed to indications of the heterosexual spread of AIDS among Africans and Haitians. Unfortunately, there are insufficient data available to statistically evaluate the impact of immigration from all areas on the spread of STDs in the United States. The value of such information would be in improving estimates of the potential demand for condoms and targeting usage programs.

Estimates of Demand

In order to estimate the potential demand for condoms, it is necessary to delete from population statistics all subgroups which are unlikely to become condom users. These adjustments are based on subjective investigations. In order to simplify this presentation, Table 7D shows each computation in arriving at an estimate.

The starting point is the population between the ages of 15 and 44 and an estimate of the number of couples this represents. (As used here, "couple" refers to the pairing of a male and female rather than any formal relationship.)

Persons not sexually active are easily eliminated from consideration. Also studies show that most sterilized individuals or those using the pill do

Table 7D. Estimates of Potential Condom Demand (Millions)

	1988	*1993*
Persons Aged 15–44	115.9	116.8
Couples Aged 15–44	58.0	58.4
Less: Those Not Exposed	–16.2	–16.4
Total At Risk	41.8	42.0
Less: Unlikely Candidates		
Sterilized	–8.1	–8.2
Pill Users	–13.3	–13.4
Subtotal Possible Users	20.4	20.4
Less: Users of Other Prod.	–5.2	–5.3
Potential Condom Users	15.2	15.1
Condom Users	–7.0	7.0
Potential New Users	8.2	8.1
Less: 30–44 Yr. Olds	–4.0	–4.4
Possibly Receptive		
New Condom Users	4.2	3.7
Condom Users	7.0	7.0
Estimated Total Potential		
Condom Demand	11.2	10.7

not consider themselves at risk of STD infection. Therefore, persons using these techniques were subtracted. Most persons using other forms of contraception are familiar with condoms and have chosen an alternative product. Consequently, the numbers representing this group are subtracted from the list of likely condom users. This leaves an estimated 15 million potential condom users. Of these seven million already use condoms. The focus is then on the eight million possible new users. Most individuals have made their choices about contraception by the age of 30. This reduces the possibly receptive target population to 4.2 in 1988 and 3.7 million in 1993 based on the aging of the population. Adding back the current users indicates that condom usage in the United States could possibly be increased 50 percent if all the potential customers became condom users. As is evident from the previous subjective analysis, capturing this market will be difficult. There has been a historic resistence to condom use reinforced by the fact that most persons in this "potential" group have not used any contraceptive or STD protection in the past.

Insights

Investigation into the data available on the consumer acceptance of condoms has provided a number of insights relative to the problems of forecasting demand.

First, much of the information available on condom usage is based on attitude surveys and focus surveys done at various times by different research organizations. As data for calculating the size of the market, many of these studies have proven to be inaccurate. A study conducted for Schmid Laboratories in October, 1987, for example, indicated that "between one-fifth and one-quarter of all men use condoms." If this information were combined with an average frequency of intercourse of three times a week as reported by other researchers, 1988 condom use would have totaled between 12 and 15 million gross, a number four to five times as large as the known sales and available productive capacity. Therefore, every value reported must be carefully checked for reasonableness against obtainable facts before it is used.

But studies such as those cited above do have value in relative terms. By comparing consumer responses obtained from similar studies during different time periods, insights can be gained as to the trend of consumer use patterns.

The results of any sampling survey are bound to be inaccurate simply due to the difficulties in finding a truly representative sample. This problem may become even more acute whenever a subliminal bias is present: some respondents, for example, may believe that their frequency of sex is more often simply based on their most recent activities. Therefore, it is usually necessary to approach an estimate from several perspectives, to test it, to use the information that makes the most sense, and to hope the conclusions are not too much in error.

Second, the demand for condoms correlates directly with population not with price. If the sexually active population is not growing, additional condom demand must be sought in converting nonusers into users via some means other than price.

Third, condom manufacturers supplied products to over 50 percent of the prospective users during 1988 and are projected to cover close to 70 percent of the potential market in 1993 without increasing sales. Thus, the outlook for the industry is for demand to remain flat. Adding new users is possible, but based on historical patterns it seems unlikely.

Chapter 8

Costs to Society

Overview

All industries exist to provide goods and/or services for consumption. Few industries have as great a potential to impact the total economy as condoms. This is especially startling given the small size of the condom industry relative to the gross national product. The importance of condoms is not found in what they cost, the size of the current demand, or the impact on employment, all of which are comparatively small. Their significance lies in the opportunity costs to society caused by many of those who are not using condoms.

If used regularly, condoms can help prevent pregnancies by those who cannot or are not prepared to support the children. In 1985 alone, the cost of childbearing by teenaged girls cost the citizens of the United States $16.7 billion. This figure is a minimal public cost and does not include other services likely to be used by families begun by a teen birth.

The direct and indirect costs of AIDS in 1986 was estimated at between $6.2 and $8.7 billion. This is just a beginning in terms of the incidence and costs associated with this dread disease.

The other STDs for which I found cost estimates, genital herpes, gonorrhea, chlamydia, and PID, add another $5.5 billion a year. Thus, today the public costs which could largely be allocated to nonuse of condoms totals over $30 billion a year.

Many of the researchers who have estimated the social costs of teenage pregnancies and STDs cite a lack of reliable data. The consensus seems to be that most of these estimates understate the true costs. This may well be the case, but for the purposes of this paper they are accurate enough to make the point: the costs associated with not using condoms are enormously greater than the $25–40 paid at retail by a sexually active couple for condoms in the course of a year.

This chapter precedes the next chapter's discussion of the profitability of the condom industry. My purpose is to provide a social benchmark against which to judge the industry's performance and assess what realistic actions might be expected from the private sector to increase usage.

Teenage pregnancies, STDs, and AIDS will be discussed separately including the available costs of each to society. These costs will then be totaled and put into perspective concerning the direction of the future outlook. My intent is to provide some understanding of the magnitude of the problem and possible options for controlling or reducing it.

Teenage Pregnancies

No reliable estimates were found of the total number of unwanted births that occur in the U.S. each year. The findings of a national survey of family growth[1] lists data for married women, but no way was uncovered to relate these births to social costs. As a result, the cost to the public for unwanted births focuses on adolescent pregnancies, a subject which has generated considerable research and published data.

Adolescents in the United States have the world's highest rates of childbearing. "About ten percent of U.S. teenagers become pregnant, and six percent give birth every year."[2] The teenage pregnancy rate is dramatically higher in the United States than in other Western nations. One-fifth of U.S. births are to teenagers. Twenty-three percent of all teenagers giving birth in 1984 were having their second, third, or fourth child.[3] Along with high unintended birth rates among adolescents, the U.S. leads other developed countries in the number of abortions.

Teen pregnancies can be traced to a number of social factors. High rates of population growth and residential mobility, the high crime rate, large numbers of teen suicides, the easy availability of sexually explicit magazines, movies, and TV programs, and a high stress level are all associated with the rate of teenage pregnancies. Large numbers of teenagers dropping out of school also correlate closely with teen birthrates.

Surprisingly, researchers have found that welfare payments do not appear to be an incentive for childbearing among black or white adolescents.

Adolescents that are black, poor, and live in metropolitan areas are particularly likely to become pregnant. Calculations by Martha Burt, published in an article in *Family Planning Perspectives*,[4] indicated a single-year cost to the U.S. public of $16.7 billion in 1985. This estimate includes monies paid through three programs—Aid to Families with Dependent Children, Food Stamps, and Medicaid—for women who first gave birth as teenagers. The U.S. taxpayer will pay, in 1985 dollars, $13,902 a year over 20 years for the family by the first birth of a teenager. For all teenage births during 1985, the 20-year total will be $5.2 billion. If all teenage births could be delayed until the mother was 20 years old, the potential saving to the public would be $5,600 for each birth and $2.1 billion for all teenage births in 1985, a 40 percent saving.

There is no one-to-one relationship between teenage childbearing and public costs. Teenage births are mostly delayed rather than eliminated, and factors associated with poverty still characterize the lives of most of the teenagers associated with unintended pregnancies. These factors usually lead to public dependency for some portion of these individuals' lives.

Eighteen years is the base period over which a teenager and her family are considered potential recipients of public support. However, because of the levels of subsequent fertility known to be associated with teenage births, there is a 30 percent chance of a second pregnancy within two years. Consequently, there is a high probability of public support being required for more than one child.

The $16.7 billion figure spent on teenage mothers in 1985 was obtained by Burt from U.S. budget estimates and includes administrative costs. The components were:

Aid for Dependent Children	$8.3 billion
Food Stamps	3.4 billion
Medicaid	5.0 billion
Total	$16.7 billion

Not included in these estimates were other services which are more likely to be used by families begun by a teenage birth than other families. Among these are: publicly supported social services, housing, special educational programs, foster care, and child protective services. Since a basis for estimating these costs is not available, the $16.7 billion is a minimum figure. Families started by a teenage birth absorb approximately 53 percent of the total public welfare expenditures.

Differences in the numbers of teen pregnancies and abortions, which are also related to teen sexual activity, occur among the states. For instance, in 1980 Mississippi had a very high teenage pregnancy rate and the highest teen birth rate but one of the lowest abortion rates of all the states. California, on the other hand, with a higher pregnancy rate than Mississippi, had only a moderate birth rate and the highest abortion rate of any state. The adolescent abortion rate in the United States is as high or higher than the birthrates and abortion rates combined in Canada, England and Wales, France, the Netherlands, and Sweden.

In 1984 56 percent of teenage births were out of wedlock. This compares to 15 percent in 1960. About 500,000 teenagers become mothers each year: the rest of the one million pregnancies a year are either miscarried or aborted. Teenage girls account for one-third of all the abortions performed in the United States. The large number of teenage mothers is one reason for the high infant mortality rate: 10.8 infant deaths for every 1,000 live births. The United States's infant mortality rate is the highest of 20 industrial countries.[5]

The obvious answer to all these problems is to get teenagers to stop having sex. However, as Dr. Sheldon Landesman, an AIDS researcher, was quoted as saying in a *Newsweek* article,[6] "After food and sleep, you are dealing with the third most powerful drive we have, and sex is the most powerful nonsurvival drive." Part of the difficulty is ignorance. From public sources at hand, young people know about sex but not necessarily what makes them pregnant. Educational programs teamed with clinics, either in the school or available locally, have shown to be effective in lowering pregnancy rates. A 1981 report[7] indicated that federal and state governments spent $285 million in 1979 to finance family planning services in the U.S. "As a result, about 695,000 pregnancies (239,000 births, 370,000 abortions, and 86,000 miscarriages) were averted among low- and marginal-income patients; and at least $570 million was saved on government expenditures during the following year for childbirth, postnatal and pediatric care, abortions and welfare payments that would have been required in the absence of these clinic services." There are numerous school clinics and about 5,000 community family-planning centers around the country. These centers recognize the pressures on teenagers, especially family problems such as unemployment, alcoholism, and suicide. The aim of the clinics is to give the teens options other than early childrearing. They need self-esteem in order to say "no." In addition, in 1973 one-fifth of the nation's colleges and universities offered birth control services, and 972 others were sending their students elsewhere for contraceptive help. (The numbers of schools and colleges offering such services is undoubtedly much higher today. Unfortunately no other data were uncovered in this study.)

Most of those young people who receive advice on contraception and free or low-cost products choose the pill. In addition, access to contraceptives is no guarantee of their use. Compliance is often a function of socioeconomic factors. Investigations by Dr. S. Emans and colleagues[8] showed that "An older, white adolescent living in a suburban household or at school, with married parents, a history of the use of other methods of contraception and a health care site in a private practice was much more likely to be compliant than an inner-city adolescent from a single parent household who received her health care in an inner-city clinic funded by Medicaid." In spite of the fact that condoms are the only contraceptive that offers protection against STDs, young women still opt for the pill.

AIDS

The impact of AIDS on public costs has been dramatic. The progression of the disease is outpacing the ability of researchers to estimate its costs with reasonable accuracy. A 1987 study by Scitovsky and Rice[9] noted both the widespread concern over the financial burdens of AIDS and the limited data available. Because of the increase in AIDS cases, the death rate from this cause is estimated to rise from 1.49 deaths per 100,000 population in 1984 to 25.74 deaths per 100,000 in 1991.

The number of persons with AIDS who were alive at anytime during

Table 8A. Estimated Economic Costs of AIDS (in Billions)

Year	Total	Direct Costs Tot.	Direct Costs Pers. Med.	Direct Costs Nonpers. Med.	Indirect Costs Tot.	Indirect Costs Morbid	Indirect Costs Mortal
1985	$ 4.8	0.9	0.6	0.3	3.9	0.3	3.6
1986	8.7	1.7	1.1	0.6	7.0	0.5	6.6
1991	16.5	10.7	8.5	2.4	55.6	3.3	52.3
		% of Total Direct and Indirect Costs					
1985	100%	20	13	6	80	5	75
1986	100%	19	13	6	81	5	76
1991	100%	16	13	3	84	5	79

Source: Anne Scitovsky and Dorothy Rice, "Estimates of the Direct and Indirect Costs of Acquired Immunodeficiency Syndrome in the United States, 1985, 1986, 1991," *Public Health Reports* 102, no. 1 (January–February 1987).

1984 was estimated at 9,368, rising to 31,440 in 1986, and 172,800 in 1991. This represents a growth in the prevalence rate from just under 4 cases per 100,000 people to almost 69 cases per 100,000 members of the population in 1991. The percentage of these afflicted individuals expected to die in the same year will range from 33 to 38 percent. The death rate from AIDS is projected to rise from 1.5 per 100,000 in 1984 to 25.7 per 100,000 in 1991.

The costs associated with AIDS can be classified as either direct or indirect costs. The direct costs include personal and nonpersonal costs. Personal medical costs include expenditures for hospital services, physician inpatient and outpatient services, outpatient ancillary services and nursing home, homecare and hospice services. Nonpersonal costs include expenditures for research, blood screening and testing, replacement of blood, health education, and support services.

Indirect costs include morbidity and mortality costs. Morbidity costs are values placed on productivity losses due to illness and disability. Mortality costs represent the present value of the future earnings lost for those who died prematurely as a result of AIDS. In their estimates Scitovsky and Rice made no attempt to include the social support services and information provided by volunteers. They also neglected to value the psychological costs due to AIDS even though they recognized that these are substantial for AIDS victims and their families. The costs estimated by Scitovsky and Rice are reproduced on Table 8A. All values are in current dollars. For 1985 the total direct and indirect costs were $4.8 billion. By 1991 the personal medical costs alone are expected to be almost twice this amount and the total direct and indirect costs almost 14 times as large. From these numbers it is easy to visualize the rapid increase in costs to society from this disease.

Of particular note are the high mortality rates. These losses of human capital are explained by the fact that most AIDS victims are young, in the 20-to-40 age bracket, and in their most productive years. Although the direct medical costs are high, they are dwarfed by the indirect costs due to premature mortality. While the authors, in their zeal for accuracy, list many deficiencies in these estimates, they serve to illustrate the tremendous burden AIDS has and will inflict upon the public. The estimated personal medical care costs of AIDS represent 0.3 percent of estimated total health care expenditures in 1986 and will grow to 1.4 percent in 1991. Similarly, when the estimated indirect costs of AIDS are compared with the indirect costs of all illnesses, they account for a 2.1 percent share in 1986 and will rise to almost 12 percent in 1991.

With all of the available data on AIDS and its tremendous impact on the young, individuals in the 15–19 year old age group are still resisting the use of condoms. Educational methods do not seem to be working. Advertising does not appear to reach this group. Fear has worked among homosexuals, but peer pressure seems to hold the most promise for adolescents. Most studies indicate that peer pressures play a substantial role in early sexual escapades. As Cheryl Walker, speaking on conditions in Southside Chicago, was quoted as saying in a *Newsweek* article,[10] "If a girl gets to be 15 or 16 years old and she hasn't had a baby yet, [her friends think] there must be something wrong with her." Perhaps peer pressure is the way to get teenagers to accept condoms. The same *Newsweek* article reported AIDS has also made boys think about condoms. While teenagers have a hard time believing in their own mortality, they are terrified of getting AIDS because someone might think they were homosexual. Promoting a macho image of using condoms may be the best, if not the only, workable approach. Perhaps as Mary Morales, director of the Hub in the South Bronx, New York, said, "maybe the best way to get the message across about contraceptives is to say use condoms—if you get AIDS, you're dead." The alternative is to wait until there are so many cases, particularly in their own age bracket, that young people can no longer ignore the threat and dramatically switch to condoms like numbers in the homosexual community have done. (Unfortunately, the implications of such a delay are both frightening and extremely costly to society.)

Other STDs

AIDS seems to dominate all consideration of sexually transmitted diseases. All STDs, including AIDS, are behaviorally correlated. The same people are at high risk: young people with multiple sexual partners, members of minority groups, inner-city residents, and the socioeconomically disadvantaged. The costs of STDs other than AIDS are high.

Pelvic inflammatory disease (PID) is the most common serious

Table 8B. Summary of Estimated Costs of PID in U.S. in 1984

Direct Costs	
PID	*$ Million*
Hospitalized Care	765
Surgical Procedures	149
Outpatient Care	151
	$1,065
Ectopic Pregnancy	
Hospitalized Care	107
Outpatient Care	3
	110
Infertility	50
Total Direct Cost	$1,225
Indirect Costs	
PID	
Outpatient	594
Hospitalized	331
Ectopic Pregnancy	68
Infertility	186
Subtotal Indirect	$1,179
Deaths	211
Total Indirect Costs	$1,390
Total Combined Cost	$2,615

Source: A.E. Washington, M.D., et al., "The Economic Cost of Pelvic Inflammatory Disease, *JAMA* (4 April, 1986).

---

complication of STDs. Every year more than one million women suffer from PID, with at least one-fourth experiencing more serious long-term sequelae. Acute PID increases the risk of recurrent PID, chronic pelvic pain, ectopic pregnancy, and infertility. The chance of ectopic pregnancy and infertility increases sevenfold after one episode of PID. Other complications occur in approximately 15 to 20 percent of the cases and often require subsequent surgical intervention. The economic burden of PID and its consequences is substantial. Nearly 300,000 women are hospitalized annually for PID, and infected women account for over 2.5 million outpatient visits every year.[11] In addition to the direct medical costs are the losses of wages and services. The majority of surgical procedures for PID occur among married women in the 25–34 age group. Infertility results in more than 20 percent of the cases. The total direct and indirect costs associated with PID as contained in an April 4, 1988, *JAMA* article[12] total $2.6 billion. This estimate is considered low because of the increasing incidences of STDs among adolescents. Sexually active adolescents are ten times as likely to develop PID as women 20 and older.

There has been a recent resurgence of primary/secondary syphilis, and chancroid and resistant gonorrhea among heterosexuals in the United States. In Oregon and New York City, for example, syphilis increased over 100 percent in 1987 compared with 1986, with blacks experiencing greater proportionate increase than whites. A 1988 study by the Centers for Disease Control pointed to a growing national problem with syphilis among inner-city drug users, prostitutes, and their sexual contacts but declines among gay men. At Gray Hospital in Atlanta, Georgia, AIDS and most STD cases among minorities have increased in the last two years but decreased among the white population. This study and ones in Connecticut and Philadelphia seem to indicate that syphilis and AIDS are likely to be ghetto diseases in ten years. These again are the groups hardest to treat and most difficult to convince to use condoms.

Dr. Willard Cates, Jr., summarized the results of studies by the National Academy of Sciences and the Institute for Health Policy studies showing estimates for the economic costs of other STDs as follows: genital herpes, $500 million; gonorrhea, $1 billion; and chlamydial infection, $1.4 billion per year.[13]

Public Support

In an editorial in *JAMA*, Dr. Willard Cates, Jr.,[14] made the case for public support of treatment of sexually transmitted diseases. The main arguments cited against government funding were:

1. Disincentive to prevention—free treatment encourages disease-prone behavior.
2. Promotes sexual irresponsibility.
3. Funds could be used elsewhere.
4. There is no public health threat—STD victims can only blame themselves.
5. Private medical care is better.

In rebuttal Dr. Cates offered the following arguments:

1. For those who cannot afford private medical care, publicly funded clinics encourage early treatment, reduce the risk of more complicated conditions developing, and provide education to reduce future episodes.

2. Moralizing serves no useful purpose. When the victim is blamed and censured, medical care is hindered, and the problem is driven underground to erupt magnified at a later time.

3. Public funds for clinical care have proven to be cost-effective. Thus, it would cost the taxpayers more not to provide treatment.

4. STDs do affect innocent victims such as the monogamous partners of infected persons and the offspring of women with genital STDs.

5. STD training has been received by less than 10 percent of the nation's physicians. Therefore specialists in STD clinics are better equipped to handle such cases than most private practitioners.

The annual total of the social costs of STDs for which data have been uncovered exceeds $30 billion. While the studies used to develop this total were performed at different times using somewhat varied techniques, making the data not necessarily uniform, the summation is valid for my present purpose: to illustrate the magnitude of the social costs of sexually transmitted disease to the American public.

Studies of welfare diseconomics are primarily concerned with the actions of individuals which have harmful effects on others in their society. In his book *The Economics of Welfare,* A.C. Pigou stated his aim as "to ascertain how far the free play of self-interest, acting upon the existing legal system, tends to distribute the country's resources in the way most favorable to the production of a large national dividend, and how far it is feasible for state action to improve upon 'natural' tendencies." With respect to condoms, we have a series of inverses of these relationships. The diseconomy arises because of persons failing to use condoms. It is lack of action which produces the harmful effects on society. This lack of responsible action on the part of some individuals causes a drain on the public resources, preventing them from being distributed in the most efficient manner.

In an article in the *Journal of Law and Economics,* Ronald H. Coase[15] argued that in order "to develop a theory adequate to handle the problem of harmful effects, factors of production should be thought of as rights. . . . If factors of production are thought of as rights, it becomes easier to understand that the right to do something which has a harmful effect (such as the creation of smoke, noise, smells, etc.) is also a factor of production. . . . The cost of exercising a right [of using a factor of production] is always the loss which is suffered elsewhere in consequence of the exercise of that right." This is clearly the situation with respect to the nonuse of condoms. In completing his argument Coase reminded us that "in choosing between social arrangements within the context of which individual decisions are made, we have to bear in mind that a change in the existing system which will lead to an improvement in some decisions may well lead to a worsening of

Table 8C. Estimates of Costs Due to Teenage Pregnancies and STDs

	$ Billion/Year
Teenage Pregnancies[4]	$16.7
AIDS[9]	8.7
PID[12]	2.6
Genital Herpes[13]	0.5
Gonorrhea[13]	1.0
Chlamydial Infection[13]	1.4
	$30.9

Note: No estimate was found for the cost of syphilis.

others. Furthermore, we have to take into account the costs involved in operating the social arrangements. . . . In devising and choosing . . . we should have regard for the social effect." Obviously, if there were some way of forcing high-risk individuals to use condoms, the monetary benefits to society would be substantial. But what of the risk to individual freedom implied by any efforts to control such a private action as sexual intercourse? Might not the risk of broader application of such interference in personal liberty be far more costly to society than the financial losses now being incurred? Coercion in such a private matter exceeds acceptable bounds in a free society. Therefore, it seems in the public interest to develop programs which promote the voluntary use of condoms. Funds spent to support such an effort can easily be justified based on the current rate of loss due to nonuse.

Insights

Most studies of external social costs deal with actions by individuals or enterprises which place a burden on the community. Smog caused by operating automobiles is one example. The government helped alleviate this problem by requiring that antipollution devices be installed on all motor vehicles and enforced this with periodic inspections. The social costs caused by the nonuse of condoms are just as substantial; but sexual intercourse is a private not a public activity. There is no way to enforce the use of condoms in a free society.

When an individual takes a risk with unprotected sexual activities, the potential economic costs to society are far greater than they are for the person involved. STD infections are personal burdens for the inflicted party, but the cost is at least shared and often completely covered by the general public. The differential between the private cost and the marginal social cost is so large that it makes comparison meaningless. The funds required to supply condoms is so low relative to the social cost that it would be cost-effective for the government to simply give condoms to the public if they would be used. Unfortunately, resistance to condom use is not a question of price or cost, but of personal preference. A totalitarian regime might be able to force the use of condoms on its citizens, but such solutions are not viable options in a free society.

The following insights have been gleaned from this survey of the available data on the costs to society of unprotected sex.

First, the opportunity cost to society, based on the failure of high-risk individuals to use condoms, is large, already approaching $30 billion a year and growing.

Second, the population segments comprising the bulk of the nonusers will be difficult to convert to condom use.

Third, easy solutions such as education, advertising, etc., have not been highly effective.

Fourth, ways must be found to reach individuals on a personal basis. For example, inner-city, ghetto-dwellers seek status and security among their peers. Therefore, they must be reached through this route. Middle-class, college students may be more difficult to influence. One approach might be to make the fear of the consequences of STDs real and personal.

Fifth, the intractability of the problem of unprotected sex and the burdens on society lead to the conclusion that only a coordinated effort by industry, educators, medical personnel, social workers, and government representatives has a chance of making some gains.

Sixth, the depth of the problem and the diffuse nature of the approaches required indicate that it is not realistic to expect another surge in the demand for condoms over the near term. Containment of the situation and gradual inroads may be the most that can be anticipated.

Chapter 9

Industry Profits

Overview

All the major condom manufacturers in the United States are parts of large, diversified corporations. Analysis of their published financial statements supplies few clues to the profitability of the condom industry. Consequently, in order to study its profits and the components of the profits, it is necessary to construct a reasonable representation as I did for manufacturing costs in Chapter 3. The same base cost numbers will be used and each element discussed separately. This approach avoids the necessity of trying to estimate a single firm's pricing and costing with precision and permits me to offer a simplified and probably clearer analysis. As before, I have made every effort to assure that the numbers are representative. All values were checked wherever possible against public information and reviewed by a number of knowledgeable professionals in the industry. The values I have used are reasonably correct and do not reflect the reported experience of any single condom manufacturer.

This analysis starts with estimating market prices and the factors affecting them. The costs used in Chapter 3 form the base for making adjustments, as discussed in the intervening chapters, and considering their effects on the long-term cost curves. My capital investment estimates will again be based on the published information on the new Safetex plant. Approximations of working capital and interest charges are developed using the published accounts of LIG (Schmid) and Carter-Wallace (Trojans). Imputed returns will be prepared for the value of the funds invested and used in the business. My purpose is to determine under what conditions the condom industry might earn profits as economists define them.

The objective of this chapter is to place the size (at producer prices) and profitability of the firms in the condom industry in perspective. This should permit an evaluation of the industry in terms of its structure and its ability to meet or contribute to the socioeconomic challenges inherent in the use or nonuse of its product.

Prices

Condom manufacturers face a relatively flat price curve. List prices may vary among producers. But, as pointed out previously, the large retail chains to whom they sell have the power to control both their own costs and the consumer prices for condoms. The retail chains control the access to the consumer needed to sell the large volumes of condoms for efficient operation of the condom dipping equipment. While these retailers may mark up prices from 60 to 225 percent (based on information in Chapter 5), they are not likely to be generous in sharing any extra margins with the manufacturers. Any differences between list and actual prices are accounted for by the many so-called nonprice competitive actions such as rebates, discounts, bill-backs, slotting allowances, etc. Thus, without collusion, the condom manufacturers have relatively little influence over price.

The current price level is based on historical policies. When the sale of condoms was restricted by law to pharmacies, Schmid and Youngs priced their condoms to provide a substantial profit for themselves and an attractive return to the druggist. They had no incentive to compete on price. Such interdependent action without collusion is typical of industries with high or very high concentrations. In his book on industrial organization, William Shepherd termed this practice "tacit collusion": "oligopolistic firms do not conspire directly . . . but a firm hints and signs . . . preferred price levels. Then all the other firms simply go along."[1] The prevailing producer price level seems to be accepted by the retailers, but professional buyers are not likely to permit any increases which erode their own margins. Likewise the condom manufacturers watch each other's actions very closely. They will match or beat any price cut which could yield a significant advantage to a competitor. In any event little long-term advantage is likely to be gained by manufacturers cutting prices, since, as shown earlier, the retailer controls the price to the consumer independent of his costs. If consumer demand is not stimulated by price cuts, why make them?

An average industry price can be calculated based on the dollar volume of retail sales in 1988 of $246 million (see Tables 4A and 5A) times 0.4 (to allow for an average 60 percent gross margin at retail as covered in the section "Prices" in Chapter 5). This sets the 1988 total condom demand at $98 million at producer prices. Dividing this figure by the 3.3 million gross of condoms sold in 1988 yields a price of $30 a gross. (The exact calculation is $29.70. However, this implies an unwarranted level of precision. The reasonableness of this estimate was verified through discussions with executives active in the industry.)

Working Capital

"Working Capital" is the term used to describe the funds required to operate a business. Working capital consists primarily of inventories and accounts receivable. This investment is related directly to sales volume. The total investment in working capital can be mitigated to some extent by using the monies of suppliers (e.g., payables for raw materials, supplies, etc.).

The level of working capital can be estimated in at least two ways. The resultant values from each approach can then be used as a check against each other. By using information from the annual reports of the London International Group and Carter-Wallace Inc. (the only public data available from condom manufacturers), their working capital can be calculated by subtracting current liabilities from current assets. Then by dividing this figure by the sales revenue in each case, it is possible to estimate the ratio of working capital to sales for these firms. (Since each firm is diversified into other businesses, the values obtained may not be strictly representative of the condom industry, but they are the best guidelines available.) The numbers obtained in this way are 27.7 percent for LIG and 35 percent for Carter-Wallace.

The second approach is to determine working capital from estimates of accounts receivable and inventories. Using the same annual reports, accounts receivable can be related to sales volume and inventories to the cost of sales. For the year ending March 31, 1988, those values were:

	Carter-Wallace	*LIG*	*Average*
Accts. Rec. (% of Sales)	20.0%	25.4%	22.5%
Invent. (% Cost of Sales)	41.7%	42.0%	41.9%

Using these average values for the condom industry calculations, I obtained the following estimates. With a $30 per gross price, sales of one million gross of condoms would produce a revenue of $30 million. At 22.5 percent of sales, accounts receivable would be $6.7 million. Inventories require an estimate of manufacturing costs to calculate. This was done in Chapter 3. Using the data in Figure 3.3—$8 per gross at the one million gross output level—inventories equate to $3.4 million. Together the two values total $10 million or 33 percent of sales revenue. Thus, both approaches yielded relatively consistent ratios.

The task of estimating working capital would be simple if it varied directly with sales at all levels of output. However, as shown by Figures 3.1, 3.2, and 3.3 in Chapter 3, fixed expenses are a significant portion of the cost of manufacturing condoms. Average unit costs are very high at low production rates. Therefore, while I will use the approach of estimating accounts receivable and inventories separately to approximate the investment in working capital, the formula for inventories will be a bit more complex than a percentage of sales. The bases for the working capital estimates are:

1. Accounts receivable vary directly with sales revenue.

Table 9A. Formula for Estimating Working Capital

1. The value for accounts receivable is taken at 22 percent of sales revenues. At a selling price of $30 per gross, accounts receivable = $6.6 per gross.

2. Inventories are based on manufacturing costs and have both fixed and variable components. Fixed charges in inventories = annual fixed manufacturing expenses less the capital consumption allowance. (The capital consumption allowance is deducted to avoid double counting. These allowances are included in the imputed returns on fixed investment if the capital investment is held constant at the original cost. An alternative would be to depreciate the fixed investment, an unnecessary complication for this presentation.)
The value becomes $4.5 − $0.7 = $3.8 million.

3. The variable cost in inventories is the variable manufacturing cost: $3.42 per gross, as shown in Table 3D.

4. Thus, working capital in $ million = 3.8 + (6.6 + 3.4) r where r = production rate in million gross.

---

2. Variable inventory costs are directly proportional to the number of condoms sold.

3. Fixed charges are constant over all levels of output. The fixed expenses were taken from Table 3D minus the capital consumption allowances.

The formula for calculating working capital estimates is shown in Table 9A.

Imputed Returns

Economic costs include a return on equity. If all monies were borrowed, it would be necessary to earn at least enough to cover the interest on this debt. Moreover, an entrepreneur would need to realize some amount in excess of the interest cost to justify the risk of being in the business. This is true whether the owner is a single individual or a group of stockholders. Economic profits are monies earned after all costs including the cost of capital have been covered.

In the example, capital costs are:

Fixed investment = $10 million (from Table 3D).

Working capital varies with sales dollars, per Table 9A.

To complete the calculations an assumed interest was taken as 10 percent a year and the minimum return for investing in this business another 5 percent. This makes the minimum imputed return $1.5 million a year plus 15 percent of the working capital.

Table 9B. Formula for Calculating Total Cost

1. *Fixed Expenses*	*$ Million/Year*
a. Fixed manufact. expense	$4.5
b. Fixed admin. expense (0.089 × 0.7 × 30)	1.9
c. Imputed return on $10 million fixed investment (0.15 × 10)	1.5
d. Imputed return on fixed portion of working capital (per Table 9A) (0.15 × 3.8)	0.6
Total Fixed Costs	$8.5
2. *Variable Expenses*	*$/Gross*
a. Variable mfg. cost (p. 42)	$3.42
b. Selling expense (0.28 × 30)	8.40
c. Imputed return on variable portion of working capital (0.15 × 10 per Table 9A)	1.50
Total Variable Cost	$13.32
3. *Total Fixed and Variable Cost*	*$ Million*
a. At 0 gross output	$8.5
b. At 1 million gross output (8.5+13.32)	$21.8

Administrative and Sales Costs

Administrative costs are generally a fixed annual charge. From the annual reports cited earlier, the relationship between administrative costs and sales can be calculated. Fiscal 1988 was a good year for both Carter-Wallace and LIG. Therefore the 8.9 percent ratio of administrative expense to sales revenue reported for this period seems a reasonable basis for calculating administrative costs at a relatively high level of output. In the example, a production level of 700,000 gross condoms equates to sales of $21 million and administrative costs of $1.9 million.

Sales and distribution expenses were taken to vary directly with sales and were set at 28.2 percent of sales revenues on the same basis used above.

Total Costs

As can be seen from the calculations shown in Table 9B, in this example total costs rise linearly with sales from a positive intercept at zero output representing fixed expenses. The resultant total cost and revenue curves are shown in Figure 9.1. From this chart it can be seen that the break-even point, where total costs equal total revenues, occurs in the example at sales of 500,000 gross of condoms per year. Below this volume the firm suffers losses. Above the break-even point volume, profits are generated. This chart graphically illustrates the high profits that can be earned in the condom industry at high market shares. Half a million gross was about 15 percent of the 1988 retail demand for condoms.

The long-run average cost curve is shown in Figure 9.2. This curve illustrates the relationships between unit costs and price.

During the 1987 surge in demand, some condom manufacturers were quoted in the press as doubling capacity. If these firms made this investment and subsequently failed to operate the facilities due to insufficient demand, the forecasted stream of income used to justify the investment would not become available. However, the cost of capital, (i.e., imputed returns which were taken at 15 percent of the original cost) would remain. Without sales no investment in working capital is necessary. Using a $10 million investment in facilities would mean a $1.5 million increase in annual costs. Returning to Figure 9.1, a new total cost line would be parallel to the one shown and would be $1.5 million higher at every level of output. This would move the break-even point to the right, to 600,000 gross.

Return on Capital Employed

Working capital computed using the formula developed in Table 9A is $13.8 million at a production rate of one million gross of condoms per year. Adding $10 million of fixed investment brings the total capital employed at this level of operation to $23 million. A profit of $8 million makes the return on capital employed 33.6 percent if this level of sales (i.e., one million gross for the values used in this example) is achieved. This is a highly attractive rate when one remembers that the total cost includes an imputed 15 percent return.

At an annual rate of 750,000 gross, working capital becomes $11.3 million and yields an 18.8 percent return. (750,000 gross would have been a 23 percent market share in 1988.) Clearly, the key to profits in the condom business is high market share.

Condom producers earn economic or monopoly profits (i.e., the amount by which the producer price exceeds the average cost, including a minimum imputed return) at operating rates in excess of the break-even level. These profits are generated in a manner different from the usual assumed route which holds that monopoly profits result from control over pricing. As I demonstrated earlier, the oligopolists in the condom industry do not control their prices. They accept the going rate. In the condom industry, monopoly profits arise from the attraction of the brands which generate sufficient sales to permit the manufacturers to take advantage of economies of scale based on high market shares. It is this combination of efficient production capability and a high level of demand relative to the total market size that makes monopoly profits possible. If there were no

Figure 9.1 Break-Even Curve for Condom Manufacturers

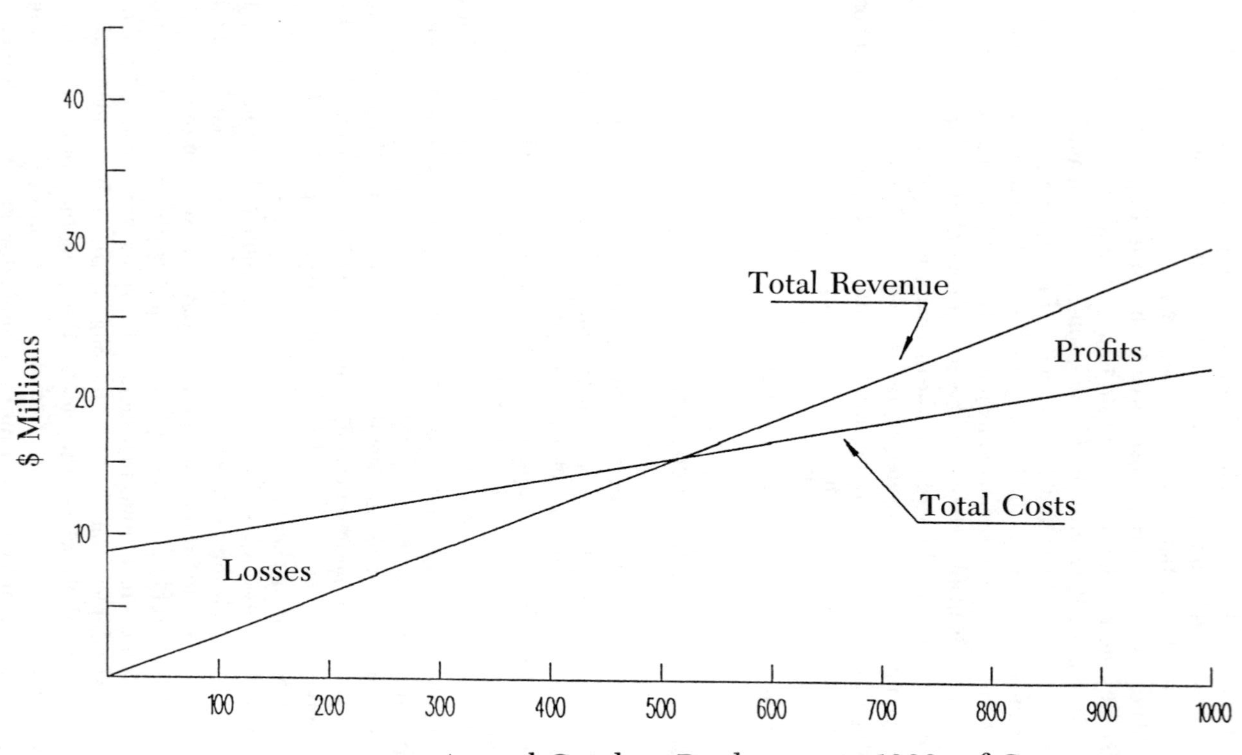

difficulty in obtaining the required high volume of sales, new producers would be attracted into this business and the monopoly profits would soon disappear. However, a high market share is required to simply break even in the condom business and—as discussed earlier—several other barriers to entry also exist. It is the combined effects which determine the oligopolistic structure and the existence of monopoly profits in the condom business.

Other Costs

Once again it is necessary to mention that the cost and profitability data presented here are a reasonable representation of the condom industry. However, these data are not taken from any current producer. There are many factors which might cause costs to be higher than those used here.

For example, as mentioned in Chapter 6, during 1987 the FDA increased its surveillance of condom quality. As a result some firms added staff to achieve better and more professional quality assurance and to affect liaison with government inspectors. This action increased fixed overhead expenses.

With better supervision of quality control, at least initially, rejects increase, adding to variable costs. The point in the manufacturing process where the rejects are found determines the level of these extra costs. Obviously, in the early stages of production each reject carries less cost. Rejected finished and packaged condoms are significantly more expensive. Products that must be recalled from retailers (defective condoms rarely reach the consumer) are not only costly because now expenses will include the handling and replacement costs, but also may injure the manufacturer's credibility. Rejects also reduce productive capacity; a 10 percent failure rate requires that 111 condoms be produced for every 100 sold.

GMP inspections add to cost by requiring careful maintenance and handling procedures. The presence of government inspectors is always disruptive even when they find nothing amiss.

Failure to keep condom dipping equipment operating continuously adds to costs several ways. First, there is obviously less throughput. Higher maintenance costs are incurred because equipment needs more frequent cleaning and more care to resist corrosion. With more frequent shutdowns comes greater material losses—latex compound can not be left in the dip tanks between runs because it will partially cure and contaminate the next run. Time is required for both the workers and the equipment to reattain an efficient running speed. In addition, many of the best workers seek employment elsewhere during layoffs, which adds to costs because experience is important in some key processing jobs. Rejects also usually rise with shutdowns. With highly automated processes, low costs are only realized when the equipment is operated in the manner for which it was designed.

Figure 9.2 Average Cost and Revenue Curves

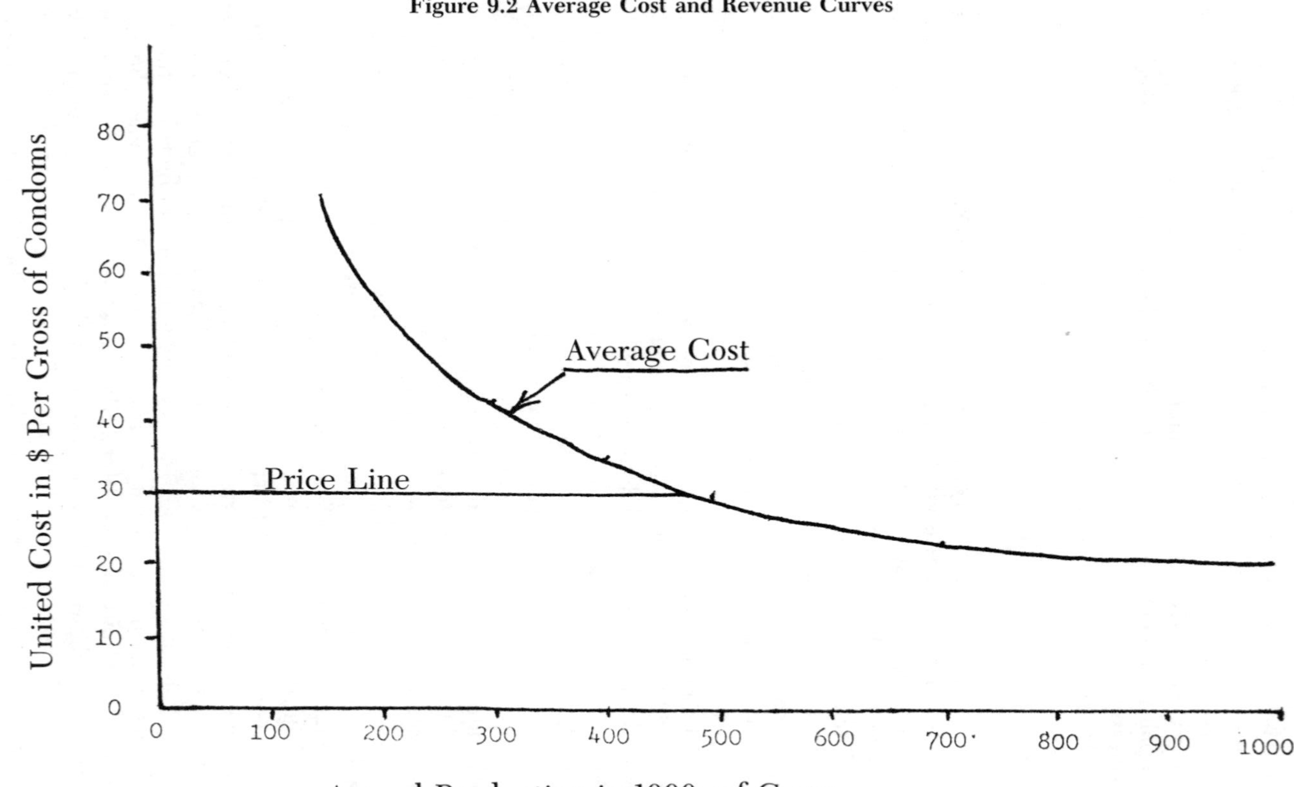

Efforts to maintain or increase market share add to costs. Experiments with national advertising, particularly TV, are very expensive. The report, cited in Chapter 5, claiming that condom manufacturers spent $23 million on advertising in 1987 can be put in perspective by looking at Figure 9.1. At an operating rate of one million gross per year, profits total $8 million. It would take the entire year's profit to pay for one-third of the ad costs. Sales of one million gross of condoms would have meant a 30 percent market share in 1987. The extent of national advertising coverage by condom manufacturers in 1987 was not great. The message is clear: the condom business is just too small to support very much TV advertising. Yet, in an effort to fend off inroads from competitors or to gain market share, some producers apparently spent more on advertising than could be justified.

In their attempts to gain new business, condom producers offer either slightly different condom shapes or colors or frequently repackage the same products to appeal to different market segments. The condoms offered in packages designed for women are an example. Even the new packaging and distribution costs can be significant if the sales of these products do not develop as planned.

While no long-term benefits can be expected from even indirect price cutting, short-term efforts to maintain market share can also dampen profits for manufacturers. Because most health and beauty aid firms use "full revenue" accounting (i.e., all sales are booked at list prices, and discounts, rebates, etc., become sales or marketing expenses), it appears that prices are maintained. However, the various incentives for customers in this case raise costs (i.e., effectively lower the price) which leads to lower profits.

In terms of the average cost curve shown in Figure 9.2, cost boosts such as those noted here move this curve toward the upper right-hand corner.

Barriers to Entry

H. Michael Mann, in his article "Seller Concentration, Barriers to Entry, and Rates of Return in Thirty Industries 1950–1960,"[2] identified four situations which yield high barriers to entry. In first place he put the importance of economies of scale where "an entrant would have to supply a substantial fraction of industry output in order to operate at the minimum optimal scale of plant or firm." The condom industry certainly meets this criterion. As shown in Figure 9.1, the break-even volume for a domestic U.S. producer is around 500,000 gross per year, a figure that represents more than 15 percent of the 1988 retail demand for condoms. Entry of a new producer at this scale would result in excess capacity in the industry. However, because of the price inelasticity of consumer demand and the oligopsonistic position of the large retailers, a price war would seem unlikely. Rather, the new manufacturer will be unable to sell enough units to be successful.

Second on Mann's list is product differentiation advantages which necessitate an aggressive marketing program in order for an entrant to overcome consumer preferences for the products of the leading firms. The established condom manufacturers command the loyalty of the regular condom users who have demonstrated a reluctance to change brands easily. Condom purchases are comparatively infrequent and represent a minor transaction to the individual. It would require an intensive program over a long period of time to induce a significant number of users to switch brands. To date, condom users have not proven to be very responsive to media advertising. In addition, retailers forecast their profits based on a combination of markup and turnover. It would take an inordinately high profit margin to induce them to relinquish valuable display space to products which do not have an established consumer following to ensure fast turnover of inventories.

Mann's other two high barriers are not applicable to the condom industry. The established condom producers do not control scarce resources. The raw materials are readily available and condom manufacturers do not represent major shares of the purchase of any of the ingredients they use. The amount of labor in condom manufacturing is small. Condom producers are relatively insignificant in terms of the number of workers employed.

The amount of capital required to build an efficient condom plant is modest compared with many other industries. Therefore, the funds required to enter this business would not represent a deterrent to a moderately financed firm. This lack of a substantial capital requirement eliminates Mann's fourth barrier.

When analyzing barriers to entry, Bain[3] and Mann found seller concentration to be a complementary contributor (i.e., the combination of concentration and barriers to entry had the greatest impact on profits). In order to determine how well the condom industry fit the findings of these researchers, I made calculations of the pretax returns on sales and equity for Carter-Wallace Inc. and London International Group (the only publicly held firms). These calculations were based on published information, as was the data used by Bain and Mann. Table 9C lists the computed values. (David Quall's publication[4] was used as the basis for this table because he used Mann's data but also added another calculation for comparative purposes, the percent return on sales.) With 83.7 percent of sales accounted for by only three firms, the condom industry clearly exceeds the minimum requirements (70 percent for the top eight firms) for a highly concentrated industry. And, as covered above, there are very high barriers to entry. Therefore, I used the values presented by Mann for firms meeting these (Bain's and Mann's) most rigorous standards for comparison. As can be seen from the data, both LIG and Carter-Wallace exceed the averages reported in these earlier studies. Only two industries in the Mann sample, nickel and sulphur, had a higher return on sales, and none reached the level of return on worth earned by the condom manufacturers.

Table 9C. Pretax Profits as % of Sales and Net Worth

Years	*LIG* % *Return on*		*Carter-Wallace* % *Return on*		*Mann Study* % *Return on*	
	Sales	*Worth*	*Sales*	*Worth*	*Sales*	*Worth*
1950–60	– –	– –	– –	– –	7.5%[1]	16.4%[1]
1984	9.4%	31.5%	[2]	[2]		
1985	9.6	27.7	10.4%	20.3%		
1986	10.7	33.2	11.5	22.8		
1987	10.7	35.1	12.0	23.5		
1988	10.4	43.5	12.6	23.0		

1. Taken from David Qualls's "Barriers to Entry and Profit Margins," *Journal of Industrial Economics* 20, no. 2 (1972) 231–242. Qualls used data from the Mann study in his paper. Since he also reported the return on sales, the Qualls data were copied for this table.
2. Carter-Wallace did not purchase Youngs's condom business until 1985.

Note: The Carter-Wallace and LIG data were based on years ending March 31.

In his investigations into differential profit rates, W. Semmler[5] reported that according to Demsetz "a persistence of (high) profit rates results not from market power as measured by concentration but, on the contrary, from higher productivity of firms in concentrated industries." Semmler also noted that "Barriers to entry are . . . no longer to be seen as determinants of the oligopolistic markets . . . but as an outcome of the activities of the oligopolistic markets themselves." These observations match the realities of the condom industry and support Semmler's conclusion that "High entry barriers . . . which deter new competitors and allow entry-preventing pricing are a necessary precondition for decreasing competition within industries." With a price-inelastic consumer demand, it is the insulation of the manufacturer from this demand that makes entry barrier pricing possible in the condom industry. If the producers had direct access to the consumers, they could charge prices high enough to make inefficient manufacturing levels profitable and possibly high advertising costs feasible. Direct access would also, however, eliminate the merchant's power over the retail price and his incentive to maintain high prices and support the oligopolistic structure among manufacturers. With direct access, the kinked demand curve would disappear along with monopoly profits.

The existence of the retailing monopsony fulfills a requirement identified by Stigler and others that there must be a postentry difference between the competitive conditions facing the new entrant and the established firms. Once an entrant has invested in a new plant he is theoretically competing on an equal basis. If there is no difference, these authors argue, there can be no real barrier to entry.[6] As von Weisaker wrote: "Economists normally implicitly assume that barriers to entry are a distortion of the competitive process. They inhibit the proper working of the principle of the 'invisible hand' and thus imply inefficiencies."[7]

The greatest barrier to entry into the condom industry is the difficulty of expanding total demand. As long as the condom industry remains small, entry by new producers will be difficult. Significant expansion of a market changes the options available to all existing or potential stakeholders. The happenings of 1987 in the condom industry provided some insights into how quickly outsiders are attracted to a fast-growing industry. At this writing the interest appears to have been short-lived, having abated with the falling growth rate of the condom business.

A class of barrier seldom mentioned in the literature but which appears in the condom industry is institutional or structural practices. Slotting allowances which prevent new entrants from access to the consumer would be an example of such a barrier. The FDA requirements that define the product and greatly restrict the firms' competitive options would also fit. Other industries would undoubtedly provide additional examples where institutional rigidities based on regulatory or trade practices effectively bar new producers from entering the market. In the case of condoms, these barriers are selective based on the characteristics of the potential entrant. Some firms would find the practices unacceptable; to others they would merely be annoyances. Firms which would not be easily deterred are those which are in related businesses like organizations already under FDA scrutiny and/or selling to the same retailers. Enterprises without these characteristics would consider the institutional barriers substantial. In his paper "Firm Decision-Making Processes and Oligopoly Theory," Paul L. Joskow discussed the lack of attention given to industry practices in organization theory. "The sick sister of the structure-conduct-performance nexus of industrial organization is the conduct part or, as I would rather refer to it, behavior. The oral tradition of industrial organization abounds with many behavioral stories about pricing, entry, research and development, financing, etc., but they have not been incorporated into our theoretical conception of industrial markets . . . the essence of the oligopoly problem is behavior."[8]

Investments and Expansion

Investment in new plants and equipment has a unique place among the factors of production in that the decision-makers exercise control over their creation. Additions to manufacturing capability may be undertaken in response to increases in demand, changes in technology, or both.

Technical innovation may be triggered by a desire to lower costs to become more competitive or to raise profits. Investing in new technology may also be based on a desire to increase or sustain demand through product improvements. Such improvements may produce demonstrably better merchandise, or they may simply be cosmetic, as illustrated by many "new" automobiles. Investments based on technology are less risky than expenditures made in anticipation of increased demand. Physical programs are measurable and controllable, but sales forecasts are speculative.

Demand may also rise based on external events such as the AIDS scare that led to a surge in condom demand in 1987. It was this growth in sales that led to consideration of increasing condom productive capacity rather than any need to lower costs or improve the product.

All investment in the fixed factors of production is justified based on expectations of a stream of future income. The more costly the equipment relative to its earning power, the longer the time period over which the future earnings must be forecasted and the greater the risk. If the cost of the investment can be recouped in one year then only twelve months—or possibly two years to allow for a return on the investment—of operations need to be projected to justify the expenditure. Most capital decisions are based on longer term expectations; usually only minor investments are recovered in one year. The choice of adding facilities depends on a manager's view of the future and his or her confidence in the potential for that vision being realized. In the past when the owners and the managers were the same individuals, the connections between risks and rewards were direct. But the U.S. condom industry is composed of publicly held corporations. The decision-makers are professional managers, who may or may not own stock in their firm, and whose main income is derived from salaries or bonuses.

Corporate investment decisions require some financial computations to justify the expenditure—if only to cover the decision-maker's tracks. There are numerous techniques used, including payback period, return on capital employed, present value, internal rate of return, etc. The most widely accepted approach is to account for the fact that future streams of income have less value than cash in hand. Therefore, the projected income streams are discounted at some acceptable rate of return to determine the present worth of the undertaking. If the calculated present value exceeds the required investment, the project is considered attractive. (The magnitude of the difference between the present value and the cost provides an indication of the risk. If the difference is small, then the forecasts used must be close to reality. Large differentials indicate there is more tolerance for errors in the estimates.) This technique, known as discounted cash flow (DCF), became popular in U.S. industry starting in the early 1960s. However, the calculation has long been used by economists. Irving Fisher used the method in figuring "the rate of return over cost"[9] in 1930 and Keynes calculated his "marginal efficiency of capital" similarly in his General Theory in 1935.[10] (These are random examples to illustrate the long use of the methodology. Its use apparently predated these authors, but this issue was not researched for this book.) However, it would be unwise to rely too heavily on the methodology. To quote a textbook in business finance published in 1958: "The very real uncertainty about economic and business conditions . . . years hence tends to reduce confidence in decision making based on literal application of precise criteria. The results are only as accurate as the underlying assumptions. . . . This is undoubtedly an important reason for the popularity . . . of the simple rule-of-thumb payback criterion. . . . This does not mean that objective analysis is valueless. What it does mean is that it does not take the place of judgment."[11] Today business is more sophisticated, and the computer has made it simple to employ discounted cash-flow techniques to analyze myriad possible scenarios. More recent writers, for example Doherty,[12] Kurtz,[13] Van-Horne,[14] Weston and Copeland,[15] present the DCF technique as the *sine qua non* of investment analysis. This is illustrated by the following quote: "The two discounted cash-flow methods—internal rate of return and net present value—are the only appropriate means by which to judge the economic contribution of an investment proposal."[16] The logic of discounting future streams of income is undoubtedly superior to the simpler methods. However, there is little evidence that these more revealing calculations have led to better decisions.

All evaluation techniques require the estimation of future streams of income. The calculations are essential, but it must be remembered that they are completely dependent on the assumptions used. The resultant numbers can be no more valid than the basis for their estimation. Because the arithmetic is precise, it often implies an unjustified level of accuracy. As Keynes pointed out "The oustanding fact (in forecasting for investment) is the extreme precariousness of the basis of knowledge on which our estimates of prospective yield have to be made. Our knowledge of the factors which govern the yield on investment some years hence is usually slight and often negligible."[17] Current approaches to risk, such as the ones used by the authors cited in the last paragraph, employ probability theories to round out the mathematical analysis of investments.

Unfortunately, few business executives deal with risk on this basis. They cannot realistically describe numerically the level of uncertainty surrounding each aspect of a project or weigh the importance of each. Nor would executives feel comfortable with the conclusions mechanically generated by such an approach. Business persons deal with issues based on their cumulative subjective analysis, reasoning, and instinct. To the extent that numerical procedures are allowed to override judgment, the risk of error may increase. Hayes and Jaikumar, writing in the *Harvard Business Review*,[18] illustrated some of the potential weakness by an example. "More than a third of U.S. machine tools . . . (are) 20 years old or older machines. Over (the 20 years) a number of investment proposals have been studied, and well meaning managers . . . decided not to replace the equipment. For many companies the cumulative effect of these decisions—each no doubt justifiable, but collectively suicidal—are an outgrowth less of a strategic plan than the normal functioning of the companies' capital—budgeting systems. . . . Once they recognize what is going on, many companies simply force new investment by short-circuiting their standard capital budgeting process . . . top management steps in . . . for making decisions."

Expectations of prospective yields are generally based on a combination of what the decision-maker feels is known for certain and what is expected to happen. The cost of equipment and its throughput under a series of conditions can usually be established with a fair amount of exactitude. Thus, estimating the manufacturing costs, at least for condoms, at forecasted levels of sales is the easy part of any cash-flow calculation. It is foretelling the levels of demand and revenues that generates the greatest amount of uncertainty. The usual assumption is that the trend of the past will continue into the future. But on what basis is this trend to be determined? How long a base period is required for justifiably extending the past into the future? The contribution of the economist to the investment analysis process is in providing an understanding of the current general business climate and the total competitive situation. The economist provides forecasts which indicate such factors as the likely size of the market, future supply conditions, price levels, competitor reactions, currency inflation/deflation rates, the cost of capital, etc. In short, the economist provides a considered view of the present and possible environment during the period in which an investment will be expected to pay off. In addition, the economist should provide the theoretical framework of the industry and the firm. It is the task of the accountants and operating personnel to explore the line-by-line outcomes of the investment operating in this environment.

Prior to 1987, condom sales were growing around 3 percent a year. In 1987 demand jumped 50 percent. Existing manufacturers were hard-pressed to keep up with orders for merchandise. The surgeon general of the United States, supported by large numbers of influential citizens and most of the news media, emphasized the importance of condoms as the only known effective protection (other than abstinence) against the transmission of STD infections, including AIDS. Knowing that large numbers of the population still were not using condoms regularly, was it reasonable to expect the growth evident in 1987 to continue, if not at the same pace at least at a level significantly higher than prior years? A further consideration was each manufacturer's concern about maintaining the firm's market position and access to the consumer while new retail outlets were opening.

These conditions deal directly with the issue of the confidence entrepreneurs and managers must have when they act based on forecasts. No one can know for certain what will happen; therefore, an element of gambling is present. To quote Keynes: "If human nature felt no temptation to take a chance, no satisfaction (profit apart) in constructing a factory, a railway, a mine or a farm, there might not be much investment merely as a result of cold calculation."[19] The dominant factor is the shakiness of the basis for most projections. No one is sure of the future, and forecasting over a normally assumed ten-year life of equipment is chancy.

An important but seldom discussed consideration in investment decisions is the actions of competitors. Few managers are willing to trust their own or their staff's judgments when competitors are expanding. The usual assumption is "The competitors must know something we don't." There is less risk in following the moves of the pack than acting independently. It seems acceptable for a manager to be wrong as long as the major competitors make the same mistake. Thus, in late 1987 and throughout 1988 all the U.S. condom manufacturers decided to add significant new capacity. Little consideration seems to have been given to the potential for considerable overcapacity resulting if the market did not continue to expand rapidly.

Managers are paid to balance the gamble with prudent expectations. The effects of possible shortfalls must be considered and the downside risks measured against the calculated rewards. One of the weaknesses of the current professional managerial system is that most managers are protected against the adverse effects of their decisions by "golden parachutes" while the upside potential rewards are extremely attractive. The burden of bad judgment is shared most severely by the shareholders and lower-echelon employees rather than the decision-maker. Persons risking their own capital tend to behave more prudently.

Another factor that effects modern management decisions is the influence of the stock market. When enterprises were owned and run by those who invested in them, investments were made for the long term. While this concept is still supposed to guide investments in facilities and equipment, managers today must consider the effects of their actions on the firm's share price. Salaries, bonuses, and even job longevity for some executives are often determined by this connection. The reactions of stockholders are not always based on careful consideration of the facts: mass psychology and emotion play key roles. Once again Keynes expressed the thought aptly when he wrote: "A conventional valuation [of shares of stock] which is established as an outcome of mass psychology of a large number of ignorant individuals is liable to change violently as the result of a sudden fluctuation of opinion due to factors which do not really make much difference to the prospective yield since there are no strong roots to hold it steady. In abnormal times in particular, when the indefinite continuance of the existing state of affairs is less plausible than usual even though there are no express grounds to anticipate a definite change, the market will be subject to waves of optimistic and pessimistic sentiment, which are unreasoning and yet in a sense legitimate where no solid basis exists for a reasonable calculation."[20] During 1987 investors rapidly bid up the price of shares of firms which made condoms. This occurred in spite of the fact that condoms were only one product line among many offered by the diversified corporations whose shares were being traded. In catering to such a volatile group, managers often make decisions based on short-run considerations, including the next bonus, rather than the long-term health of the enterprise.

For the condom industry, high expectations can be traced to analysis of the available facts: condoms are the only effective means of preventing the transmission of STD infections, and there are large numbers of persons not using condoms who should be using them. Unfortunately, for many industries, not just the condom industry, there is a wide gap between what people logically should do and what they actually do. Another factor in misreading the market was the inadequacy of information or misunderstanding of what caused the market growth of 1987. The data seem to support the conclusion that a large portion of the increased condom sales were to homosexual men. After a large percentage of this segment of the population became condom users, the growth in demand leveled off considerably. Forecasting behavior is always risky. Projections of behavior are suspect because of the large numbers of individual options which must be accommodated. Most human beings change their habits slowly, if ever. Forecasting the reaction of individuals is best approached over a long-term trend, considering but not unduly weighing unusual dramatic changes in personal conduct.

Keynes predicted the outcome: "It is probable the average results of investments even during periods of progress and prosperity, have disappointed the hopes which prompted them. Business men play a mixed game of skill and chance, the average results of which to the players [managers] are not known to those who take a hand [investors]."[21]

The growth of the condom market eased in 1988, and demand is not presently rising. Consequently, any funds spent on expansion since 1987 are unlikely to be currently productive. The present level of condom sales is well within the productive capacity that was in existence prior to 1987, provided there are no sizeable product recalls by the FDA. A surge in demand seems unlikely to happen. The result of idle investment is that the break-even level of output is raised and sales must be increased substantially to cover the cost of the added capital. If manufacturers attempt to operate the new equipment without sufficient sales to justify such operation, costs will be even higher and losses are likely to occur.

Competitive Advantage

In his popular book *Competitive Advantage,* Michael E. Porter listed five competitive forces that determine an industry's profitability: "the entry of new competitors, the threat of substitutes, the bargaining power of buyers, the bargaining power of suppliers, and the rivalry among competitors."[22] He went on to state that "Industry profitability is not a function of what the product looks like or whether or not it embodies high or low technology, but of industry structure. . . . The five forces determine industry profitability because they influence the prices, costs, and required investment of firms in an industry—the elements of return on investment."[23] For the condom industry, three of these forces need little independent consideration. Potential entrants are discouraged by the size of the market, an entry-deterring price, and the power and self-interests of the oligopsonists. Factor costs are too small a portion of total costs to be controlling. Rivalry among established producers is restrained by institutional rigidities which make price competition impractical. Substitute products, such as the pill, have had a major impact on the total demand for condoms in the past. It is only the condom's unique advantage as a means of protecting against the transmission of STDs coupled with the fact that there is no known cure for AIDS that, as of this writing, makes the condom industry currently immune from erosion due to substitutes. The dominant factor in terms of profitability in the condom industry is the imposing bargaining power of the retailers (buyers).

Porter went on to point out "that satisfying buyer needs is at the core of success in business endeavor."[24] "The power of buyers determines the extent to which they retain most of the value created for themselves."[25] In the case of condoms, the oligopsonistic retailers retain this advantage while providing the oligopolistic manufacturers with sufficient incentive to operate an efficient supply system.

Porter considers the basis for above-average profits to be the existence of a "sustainable competitive advantage" which he went on to define as "low cost or differentiation."[26] At this point the use of this analysis technique starts to become a bit less straightforward. For condoms no physical differences between products exist. Little absolute cost advantage can be gained once the threshold production volume has been passed. The sustainable advantage is one of differentiation, but it is a difference which arises from a combination of factors. First is the consumer's preference for certain products which leads to faster turnover of merchandise at retail. Second is the recognition by the retailers that it is in their own best interest to support only a small number of brands. Finally it is the control position of the retailer (buyer) which makes it possible to maintain the discipline which perpetuates the industry structure. It is the interaction of these forces which permits the existing producers to earn monopoly profits on a sustainable basis. It is not a question of comparative cost or product advantages among the established product leaders.

A condom firm may conceivably lose its competitive advantage through errors in managerial judgment that alienate the retailers, but otherwise it is relatively protected from direct attack by new entrants.

Porter's "value chain,"[27] which he uses to analyze a firm's competitive advantage, is more of a prescription for the efficient operation of any business than a means of providing a unique edge in the condom industry. This is primarily due to the fact that condom manufacturers do not have access to the ultimate consumer. For condoms the value-chain principles are ways to determine areas for improving profits, not ways of gaining on a competitor.

Insights

The major insights from this study of the profitability of the condom industry are:

First, the condom industry is small, with only $98 million in revenues at producer prices in 1988. This has a strong influence on the market structure of the industry and the competitive actions available.

Second, the condom industry, like most oligopolies, can be highly profitable for the established manufacturers.

Third, large relative market shares must be captured and maintained in order for the manufacturers to operate at production levels which generate profits. These profits are directly related to the efficiency of the continuous dipping equipment. This is illustrated by the fact that in my example of 1 million gross per year production, manufacturing costs represent roughly 25 percent of the total revenue, while at an operating rate of 500,000 gross the unit manufacturing cost is more than 40 percent of the sales price for condoms. This reinforces not only the oligopolistic nature of the industry but also the necessity of this structure for profitable operation. If the industry were composed of many competitors and characterized by vigorous price competition, monopoly profits would disappear. But the total market is insufficient to support a large number of competitors, each having a small share.

Fourth, the absolute levels of profits in the condom industry are not large. This is a function of the size of the total market. Therefore, condom manufacturers cannot afford many of the expenses, like TV advertising, that other industries handle as a matter of course. It further serves to increase the dependence of the manufacturers on the retail distributors and point-of-purchase exposure to the consumer. A low level of total profits greatly restricts the effective options a producer has in using nonprice competitive strategies.

Fifth, condom manufacturers face a flat price line for all practical purposes. List prices may vary, but the relative lack of strength of the manufacturers causes these to be eroded by give-backs of various types to the retail distributors.

Sixth, economies of scale, an entry-discouraging price level, and consumer brand preferences are barriers to entry which provide U.S. condom manufacturers with the ability to maintain the oligopoly and earn monopoly profits during periods of peak demand.

Seventh, investment in fixed equipment and facilities is always risky. It becomes more so when there is an abnormal change in demand. Such surges, when publicly recognized, increase pressure on management to react to conditions that they had not previously experienced. As a result of circumstances of this type, some condom manufacturers increased productive capacity based on expectations of growth which did not materialize. Therefore, excess capacity now exists.

Eighth, the small size of the condom industry greatly limits its ability to assume a major role in helping reduce the social burden caused by the nonuse of condoms. Certainly there is more than adequate manufacturing capacity available, and enough condoms can be produced to fill all conceivable needs. But condom manufacturers do not have the resources needed to make a significant impact in stimulating added demand except as participants in a broad coalition.

Chapter 10

Summary and Conclusions

Overview

The introduction to this study outlined a number of tasks. My primary effort was to describe each segment of the condom industry and show how it matches the characteristics used to define an oligopoly. My work also provided insights relative to retail distribution and consumer pricing which have a direct effect on the condom industry. Beyond this I explored the sizeable socioeconomic impact that nonuse of condoms has on the national economy. Sales revenues, costs, and profits were estimated to provide a framework for judging the capability of the condom producers to contribute to alleviating some of the problems caused by unprotected sex.

This chapter summarizes these findings and offers some thoughts on their significance.

Industry Structure

The U.S. condom industry is clearly an oligopoly. The three largest condom manufacturers in the United States account for 82.2 percent of the retail market. The two leaders, Carter-Wallace and Schmid Laboratories, together hold 74.3 percent of the market. This hold on consumer sales was developed during a time when open display or advertising of condoms was illegal. Schmid and Carter-Wallace built a relationship with druggists which led to their dominance of this product category. Today, drugstores still account for two-thirds of retail condom sales and the consumer confidence engendered in the leading brands during the early years still continues. It is this consumer confidence that has permitted such dominant market positions to be maintained.

The total U.S. market for condoms is not large whether measured in terms of total dollar sales or physical units. Only one condom is used in each instance of sexual intercourse, and only about 12 percent of the couples in the sexually active age bracket of 15–44 use condoms. Average usage has been estimated at 50–75 per couple per year. (This checks fairly closely with the total number of condoms produced in 1988.) Condoms are made by dipping forms into a bath of natural rubber latex. The equipment to perform this task operates continuously and produces large numbers of condoms. The combination of a small market, high volume equipment, and an entry-deterring price leads to the requirement that a manufacturer must capture large shares of the market in order to operate efficiently, thereby satisfying another requirement for an oligopoly.

Chain store merchants, particularly druggists, control access to retail condom customers. These organizations are many times larger than the condom manufacturers. In addition, condom sales represent a tiny portion of each store's volume. As a result, the condom manufacturer has no influence over the retail price of its products and little bargaining power with the professional buyer. At the same time, because of the small number of competitors, manufacturers know that any price decrease would not increase sales because it would immediately be matched. Consequently, again characteristic of an oligopoly, both a kinked demand curve and for all practical purposes a flat price line characterize the condom industry.

One of the contributions of this study was to demonstrate that the oligopolistic price level was arrived at based on the historical development of the industry and a strategy of forestalling new entrants. This was one point not covered in Paul Sweezy's paper describing the kinked demand curve. Another contribution was to show the effect of the structure of one industry, in this case the distribution sector, on determining the market structure of another (i.e., condom manufacturing).

Because price competition is impractical, condom manufacturers compete using other techniques. Media advertising has not proven particularly effective. The use of TV advertising may well be too expensive for condom manufacturers on any consistent basis. Packaging and point-of-sale displays have received the greatest emphasis and appear to be serviceable means of reaching the consumer. The various schemes to cut prices indirectly, the so-called nonprice competitive actions, rarely have any long-term impact since they are quickly matched by rivals. Consumer confidence, brand identification, and convenient availability remain the most effective means of reaching both the consumer and the retailer.

Barriers to Entry

A number of barriers keep new firms from manufacturing condoms in the United States. Most of these would not be difficult for a well-financed, determined competitor to overcome. However, taken collectively they pose a substantial impediment to new entrants. Probably the greatest barrier is the small size of the industry. With only $98 million in sales at producer prices in 1988, a prospective entrant would have to question the size of the incentive in relation to the risk. The capital and technology requirements for the condom business are sufficient to make entry by a small entrepreneur impractical. Thus, only midsize to large firms need be considered. The charts in Chapter 9 showed that a producer operating a single plant at a volume of one million gross per year, 30 percent of the retail market, would earn $8 million on an investment of $23.8 million. This is a highly attractive rate if there were some way of capturing such a large share of a market dominated by two well-established competitors. If sales are less than 500,000 gross per year (15 percent share) losses are incurred. It would require a very confident competitor to start a new venture manufacturing condoms under these conditions. Because of worldwide production, this barrier would not apply to overseas producers.

Brand recognition is extremely important because of the consumer confidence that has come to be identified with it over the years. The cost of condoms is a very minor expenditure for a consumer. Therefore, he or she is not likely to shop primarily on the basis of price. Moreover, many consumers equate low prices with inferior quality. This retail price inelasticity increases the confidence in the brand. Because of the general ineffectiveness of condom advertising, inroads by competitors are more likely to develop from mistakes by producers which undermine consumer confidence or lead to loss of exposure at the retail level. Consumers are reluctant to experiment with less well known brands as long as their preferred product is available. There is considerable uncertainty as to consumer reaction if their brand of condom were removed from sale or became difficult to find.

Manufacturing condoms requires experience and skill as well as equipment. This is true of most products based on natural materials and subject to the variations caused by changes in soil, weather, etc. It is generally possible to hire skilled individuals and purchase the necessary equipment, but it is not easy. Even well-run existing plants have trouble making condoms from time to time, as demonstrated by the product recalls by the FDA. Producing condoms is not so difficult that the technology would deter a determined competitor, but once again the cost and risk must be judged in the context of the size of the business and the challenge of capturing market share.

As producers of a life-saving medical device, the condom industry is highly regulated. Product and facility inspections by the FDA are standard procedures. Government regulation would not be a deterrent to a firm, such as a pharmaceutical company, which is accustomed to such procedures, but it would be a discouragement for most others.

Macroeconomic Importance

The small size of the condom industry belies its potential importance. Condoms are the only effective protection against STDs for multipartnered, sexually active people. Consequently, they can help avoid some of the suffering and high costs associated with sexually transmitted disease, particularly AIDS. The financial burden of teenage pregnancies should also be considered. While other forms of contraceptives are available, they do not protect against infection and the sexual activities of most teens expose them to STDs.

Every year the U.S. government spends $30 billion to cover the costs incurred by teenage pregnancies and to treat individuals suffering from sexually transmitted diseases. This burden on the taxpayer grows annually.

When the low price of a condom is compared with the high social cost of nonuse, the case for increasing condom usage is made. The challenge is to get those at high risk to use prophylactics. The problem is not one of ignorance. Most people know about condoms, but a majority simply do not like to use them. It is not a matter of education: most college students prefer the pill to the condom. The task, as it has been with contraceptives in general, is to find a way to appeal to each individual's selfish self-interest. This implies a very extensive program, tailoring approaches to appeal to many different subgroups. No universal appeal has yet been uncovered.

Can condom manufacturers realistically help? They have an important commercial stake in the success of such an effort. They can provide condoms and some financial support could legitimately be classified as sales or marketing expense. But the condom manufacturers are too small to bear a major role. The best that can be hoped for is that the condom manufacturers will look to their own self-interest and become active partners in seeking to entice more high-risk individuals to use condoms.

Other Insights

The condom industry provides a good basis for illustrating economic principles. It is relatively uncomplicated without being simplistic. For example:

First, it provides a good case for showing how an industry evolves into a particular market structure based on its historical development. The condom industry did not originate as an oligopoly: it became one based on the interplay of a complex set of competitive, governmental, and social forces.

Second, study of the condom cost curves demonstrated the inadequacy of the classical definition of the long-run cost curves. If all factors of production are completely variable, there can be no cost curves. Costs are defined items, and they can not be specified if the basis under which they are measured is constantly changing. Since in the short run the technical factors that define the cost curve are fixed, it follows that any curve which purports to encompass all the short-run curves must also be fixed. There is little or no meaning to a cost curve that is at all points above the price line; no rational producer would ever build a plant to operate under conditions where he could never even break-even. Manufacturers often operate at a loss when circumstances force them to move backward along an existing cost curve. They will only continue to operate at a loss as long as the price is greater than their variable cost (i.e., while it is cheaper to run than to shutdown). The current definition of a long-run cost curve describes an historic trend line of minimum costs rather than a true cost curve.

Realistically a long-run cost curve is more appropriately defined as the summation of the short-run cost curves over a period of time in which successive technical changes can be made to reach the lowest possible average cost. The long-run curve is not tangential to the individual curves. Rather, it is a new curve which includes the cost components of all the short-run additions. If a new productive unit replaces a prior one, then a new cost curve must be drawn covering the complete production range, not just the section where the new increment is added. It makes no sense to use cost curves to describe nonexistent operations. Another important factor is to realize that movement in the output-curtailing direction will not precisely track the cost curve developed during the expansionary cycle. When output is increasing, economies related to scale are developed. During contractions diseconomies and problems not encountered previously continually arise.

Third, not all industries have direct access to the consumer. In such cases the manufacturer may have little or no influence over the retail price. The demand for condoms is price inelastic, yet the condom manufacturer faces a fixed price line.

Fourth, commodities whose total costs are a small fraction of a consumer's income tend to have price inelastic demands. With annual expenditures of $25–$40 per user, the incentive to buy less expensively is low. Thus, condoms represent a good example of this economic axiom.

Fifth, consumer preferences often have little to do with actual product differences. It is what the consumer perceives, not any objective measure, that determines retail choices. Condoms represent a good example.

Sixth, list prices are not always meaningful measures of true prices. Industries use a variety of schemes which reduce the cost to the purchaser without publicly cutting prices. These actions are seldom apparent from published statements of accounts.

Seventh, in most economic discussions the role of government regulation usually focuses on antitrust actions or interstate commerce. The regulation of the condom industry illustrates how the government, in this case through the FDA, often directly affects the product, the manufacturing cost, and the competitive options.

Eighth, the information available to make decisions, even after extensive study and analysis, is far from perfect. Information extracted from surveys must be carefully cross-checked against other more reliable information to be sure it makes sense. Data in the social sciences are never accurate; our hope is that they are close enough to the truth to be useful and not misleading.

Ninth, economic enterprises have roles in contributing to the general welfare as well as earning a profit for their investors. The social costs of the nonuse of condoms are many times larger than the total revenues of the condom industry (measured in either producer or consumer prices). Consequently the condom industry has a substantial contribution to make to society.

Tenth, investment in fixed equipment and facilities is risky. It becomes more so when there is an abnormal shift in demand. The happenings in the condom industry as a result of the surge in demand in 1987 provide a good example of the effects of a misreading of available information and the pressures of external forces. The erroneous investment decisions made in the condom industry also serve as examples of the "following the pack" philosophy of many executives and the fact that the burden of most bad decisions falls most heavily on owners and employees who did not participate in or influence the decisions. Top executives are usually well protected and have little incentive to be prudent.

Eleventh, monopoly profits do not necessarily depend on the control of prices. Condom manufacturers have little influence on prices. They accept the going rate, which is based on historical developments and is kept low enough to discourage new domestic manufacturers. Monopoly profits in this industry result from the combined effects of economies of scale and substantial barriers to entry.

Twelfth, failure to understand and continue the policies which led to the historical success of a business place it at risk. The condom recalls and plant shutdowns ordered by the FDA in 1987 prove that some condom producers were not paying sufficient attention to selling the reliable products on which the industry was built. When this happened in the automotive and consumer electronics businesses sizeable market shares were lost to foreign manufacturers. Hopefully, while the FDA's actions were costly they were also timely enough to alert the industry to the need to produce quality products which will continue to deserve the public's confidence.

Conclusions

Economic industry studies have an important, often overlooked, role in educating business executives. Case studies attempt to broaden experience by acquainting students with a variety of business situations. But case studies lack the depth of coverage possible with an industry study. Management skills may be transferable and there may be common elements among industries, but the ways these elements come together are often unique to each business. It is only by separating and studying each component and then putting them together in their proper interrelationship that it is possible to fully understand the success factors peculiar to that industry. While many business educators decry the short-term perspectives of business managers, they foster such an approach by teaching the subject with excessive reliance on tools which do not explore the issues deeply enough, such as case studies and computer programs. Special situations and quick answers are stressed rather than in-depth evaluation based on all the relevant internal, external, and historical facts. (The popular sport of extensive number crunching is not in-depth analysis.) I do not advocate paralysis by analysis or mean to impune a training method that has proven of value. Fast decisions are often essential in business, and it is not always possible to obtain all the facts we would like to obtain. However, such judgments should be grounded in a thorough understanding of the business, its past history, and how it operates. Too few modern executives appear to have taken this important step. They consider superficial information adequate in managing sizeable assets owned by other people and entrusted to their care. There is much to be said in support of the manager who started in the mailroom or its equivalent and worked through all operations before attaining the presidency. Owners who built their own enterprises usually have this depth of knowledge.

Today we rely on business-school training and often move managers from one industry to another. This is a valid approach only if the executive takes the time and effort to thoroughly learn the business in which he is expected to function. Each person is the product of his or her own past. It is no different with industries. Most of the U.S. businesses which have declined did so because their leaders either did not understand or forgot why they had originally been successes. Ford pioneered reliable, inexpensive motor vehicles and suffered when these principles were displaced by a management that believed that current success was due to their own marketing cleverness and the earlier emphasis on quality and manufacturing was unimportant. Now Ford is spending large sums to convince the public they have rediscovered quality. Meanwhile they have lost market share. This is not a plea to continue to make buggy whips because that was the firm's original business. Rather, I wish to stress the importance of studying an industry's development and comprehending the forces at work in the past and present as well as those likely to shape the future. The more cognizant we are of all aspects of an industry, the more likely bad decisions will be avoided.

The condom industry is an interesting case to illustrate the value of understanding all the internal and external factors that shape and operate on a business. It fits all the generally accepted requirements for describing an oligopoly but often in ways that are different from the expected norm:

1. Condom producers are price takers.

2. Monopoly profits arise from manufacturing efficiencies not market control.

3. The structural control is an external countervailing force, not one exercised by one or more members of the industry.

4. The oligopoly results in the most efficient organization.

Condom manufacturers do not have the ability to control the market as was once evident in such highly studied oligopolies as the steel and automobile industries. Condom manufacturers cannot dictate prices or sales conditions to retail merchants. No price or supply collusion is present in the condom industry. Collusion, which is often associated with oligopolies, is not likely to occur, and it could not be effective if it were tried. Control over the market rests with the distribution channels not with the condom manufacturers.

The level of consumer demand for condoms is price inelastic, but the manufacturer has no way of capitalizing on this fact. The strong intermediary position of the retailers and the large size of the store chains limit the realistic options available to the producer. Total demand is essentially fixed, and the price paid to the manufacturer is controlled by the retailer. Failure to recognize these realities can and often does lead to wasted effort. Condom manufacturers cannot change the fundamental facts of the business. They can and must be quick to keep competitors from encroaching on their share of access to the consumer, but this need not be as expensive as trying vainly to change market conditions with a low probability of success. The established condom manufacturers waste resources trying to outflank each other in a basically static situation. Their guiding principles should be to utilize their marketing exposure to retain old customers and attract new ones while preventing new entrants, particularly foreign producers, from gaining access to consumers.

Few modern executives take the time to chart total and average cost and revenue curves. Such exercises are considered irrelevant to those with reams of computer printouts of detailed information. Unfortunately, such an attitude prevents understanding of the overall mechanisms at work. Numerical analysis indicates that manufacturing costs are a minor portion of total costs at high volume and fine tuning of operations may not be cost effective. This reasoning could lead to overlooking the fact that it is the existence of economies of scale that make the monopoly profits possible in this business, not any clever marketing ploy. The cost curves also serve as a reminder of the importance of high-volume continuous operation to the continued health of the firm. Any action which curtails output will have greater-than-proportional effects on earnings and on management's flexibility to take action in other functional areas. If income is not being generated, overhead expenses can not be absorbed, which in turn will limit actions which could increase the future upside potential. Likewise, cost curves help keep the effects of adding new manufacturing facilities in proportion. Capital expenditures increase the production level required to break-even while offering attractive returns if high sales can be attained. The curves show diagramatically the effects if these goals do not materialize.

The condom industry is capable of earning monopoly profits but not because of any control over price. High profits are based on a combination of high market shares in a small industry. High shares are essential for efficient operation of automated equipment. Understanding this fact leads to the conclusion that the business can be highly attractive to firms, such as international companies, which already have a base manufacturing demand. New domestic producers would require too high a market share to break-even while foreign producers base their strategies on worldwide rather than national sales.

Youngs (Carter-Wallace) and Schmid built their strong market positions based on filling a need for a reliable product. Customers have demonstrated a willingness to pay a comparatively high price for products on which they can rely. The recalls and plant closures of 1987 demonstrate that some executives lost sight of this basis for past success. Over the short run managers thrive or fail due to the actions of their predecessors. The length of time varies but often executives are not responsible for most of the events during their tenure. Reputations for quality are particularly enduring in protected markets like condoms. It would take a major scandal for the established condom brands to be damaged significantly. However, eventually the public realizes when merchandise is inferior. Hopefully, the condom manufacturers were able to correct any inadequacies before enduring damage occurred. If this had been a more highly competitive business, the results could have been disastrous.

Information is never perfect. The common assumption that the inertia of the marketplace will cause demand to continue to rise or fall depends not only on the current data but also on some historical perspective. When a market has traditionally grown at around 3 percent a year and then jumps 50 percent in one year, projection of the one-year trend or even unduly weighing its effects is dangerous. This can lead, as in the case of condoms, to erroneous and costly decisions. What is particularly disturbing is all the major condom manufacturers expanded their production capability. This lack of prudence may well be ascribable to the fact that professional managers have much to gain and little to lose in risking the shareholder's money; the upside bonuses are attractive and the downside is protected by a "golden parachute." Any penalties for unwise moves are shifted to those with little or no influence on the decision: stockholders and lower-level employees.

All industries exist to fill the needs of society. It is in understanding these needs that insights are provided into opportunities for future expansion. The condom industry is small but has a big socioeconomic role to play relative to the prevention of STD infections. How the industry can best capitalize on this essential need has yet to be determined. The first steps toward success are recognizing the extent of the opportunity and the capabilities and deficiencies of each group within society with a stake in finding a solution. Understanding this extent is only possible based on detailed systematic research of the industry.

Based on past history the condom manufacturers are unlikely to do much to expand the use of their own products. Past successes have often been at the expense of the mistakes of others, such as the perceived health problems with the IUD and the pill. The condom producers had nothing to do with the surge of condom use of 1987. Therefore, condom producers can be expected to be reactive to situations beyond their control. Shifts of market shares within the industry are more apt to be triggered by mistakes by one of the established firms than by any marketing campaign from an aggressive competitor.

The condom industry has provided a good example of the value of economic industry studies and a means of illustrating a number of microeconomic principles which became evident under circumstances and in ways that are different from those generally described in textbooks of economic theory. Therefore, this study helps to broaden the understanding of economics as it relates to oligopolies in general as well as specifically to the condom industry.

Notes

Chapter 2

1. D. Kennedy, *Birth Control in America,* 21, 110.
2. M. Sanger, *Woman and the New Race* (New York: Brentano's, 1920), 138.
3. Lee Rainwater, *Family Design: Marital Sexuality, Family Size, and Contraception* (Chicago: Aldine, 1965), 211.
4. T. Roosevelt, "Race and Decadence," *Outlook,* 8 April 1911, 765.
5. The preceding was reported in Kennedy, *Birth Control in America.*
6. *United States Code Annotated,* vol. 18, secs. 334, 396 (1927).
7. Now *18 U.S.C. 1461, 18 U.S.C. 1462, 19 U.S.C. 1305.*
8. This history of the Killian Rubber Company was obtained during an interview with Joseph Killian, son of Burkhardt Killian, on December 27, 1988. Joseph Killian spent his business career in the condom business, retiring in 1975, when a subsequent owner of the Killian Latex plant, Akwell Rubber, sold the condom facility to Ansell Corp. He then restarted Killian Latex as a latex compounder. In 1987, well into his seventies, Joseph Killian led his company back into the manufacture of condoms.
9. Based on an interview with Phillip Frank, retired director of medical marketing and former member of the board of directors of the Youngs Rubber Company.
10. *Youngs Rubber Corporation* v. *C.I. Lee and Co., Inc.* 45F 2d 103 (1930).
11. *United States* v. *One Package of Japanese Pessaries,* 86F 2d 737 (1936), reprinted in Morris Ernst and Alexander Lindey, *The Censor Marches On,* (New York: Doubleday, Doran, 1940), 165, quoted in Kennedy, *Birth Control in America,* 7.
12. Howard Shapiro, *The Birth Control Book* (New York: St. Martin's Press, 1988).
13. Forrest and R.R. Fordyce, "U.S. Women's Contraceptive Attitudes and Practice," *Family Planning Perspectives* (May–June 1988): 117.
14. Donald H. Merkin, *Pregnancy as a Disease* (Port Washington, N.Y.: Kennikat Press, 1976).

Chapter 3

1. Robert Mauser, ed., *The Vanderbilt Latex Handbook* (Norwalk, Conn.: R.T. Vanderbilt Co., 1987).
2. *Ansell,* a report published by Ansell International (Australia, 1987).
3. *Carter-Wallace Annual Report for Year Ending March 31, 1988.*
4. *London International Group Annual Report of Accounts 1988.*
5. Roger Schraffler, "Fuji Plans 2nd U.S. Condom Plant," *Rubber & Plastic News,* January 1988.

6. Paolo Sylos-Labini, *Oligopoly and Technical Progress* (Cambridge: Harvard University Press, 1969).

7. Joel Doan, "Statistical Cost Functions of a Hosiery Mill" in *Microeconomics: Selected Readings,* 3d. ed., edited by Edwin Mansfield (New York: W.W. Norton & Co., 1979).

8. The reasonableness of this estimate was checked against the price paid by the U.S.A.I.D. for condoms from Ansell in 1986 and 1987 (i.e., 4.27 cents each). Subtracting 37.6 percent from 5.5 cents (i.e., $7.90 per gross as calculated in Table 3E) to cover packaging cost savings yields a net cost of 3.5 cents. A 1.27 cent (36.3 percent) markup is a reasonable return on bulk sales to the government.

9. Sylos-Labini, *Oligopoly and Technical Progress.*

10. Jacob Viner, "Cost Curves and Supply Curves," *Zeitschrift für Nationale Ekonomic:* Vol. 3 (1931), reprinted in Chen Fu Chang, "The Firm's Long-Run Average Cost Curve," *Quarterly Review of Economics and Business* (Winter 1969): 80–84.

11. "The Firm's Long-Run Average Cost Curve," Chen Fu Chang, *Quarterly Review of Economics and Business* (Winter 1969): 80–84.

12. A. Ross Shepherd, "Notes: The Firm's Long-Run Average Cost Curve," *Quarterly Review of Economics and Business* (Spring 1971).

13. Giora Hanoch, "The Elasticity of Scale and the Shape of Average Cost Curves," *American Economic Review* (June 1975): 492–97.

14. Charles Revier, "The Elasticity of Scale, the Shape of Average Costs, and the Envelope Theorem," *American Economic Review,* (June 1987).

15. Bruce R. Beatie and C. Robert Taylor, *The Economics of Production* (New York: John Wiley & Sons, 1985).

16. John W. Rowe, "Short-Run, Long-Run, and Vector Cost Curves," *Southern Economic Journal* 37 (January 1971): 245–50.

17. William A. Kelly and Donald M. Waldman, "A Generalized Economic/Uneconomic Boundary for Short-Run Product and Cost Curves," *Atlantic Economic Journal* 4 (December 1982): 82–85.

18. Rulon Pope, "The Generalized Envelope Theorem and Price Elasticity," *International Economic Review* 21, no. 1 (February 1980): 75–86.

19. Yves Balasko, "Equilibrium Analysis and Envelope Theory," *Journal of Mathematical Economics* 5, no. 2 (September 1978): 153–72.

20. Robert W. Mitchell, "Long-Run Cost Curves: A Comment," *Journal of Industrial Economics* (November 1971): 77–79. This article presents a refinement for Shepherd's article, reference 12 above.

Chapter 4

1. *Clinica,* no. 305 (22 June 1988): 3.

2. *Dun & Bradstreet Report,* "National Sanitary Laboratories," 19 December 1988.

3. Estimate based on discussions with competitors and suppliers.

4. *Drug Store News,* 12 December 1988.

5. "Chains vs. Independents: A Decade of Change," *Drug Store News,* 13 April 1987.

6. "The 1987 Annual Report of the Chain Drug Industry," *Chain Store Age,* 13 April 1987.

7. Ibid.

8. *Mass Market Retailers* (New York: Racher Press, 1987).

9. Tom Hornacek, Pinny Food Centers, Pincoming, Michigan; reported in *Supermarket Business/NFB,* May 1987.

10. Michael Atmore, "NFM's Exclusive Report on Space Allotment, Turns, and Promotion Paints a Picture at Retail," *Non-Food Merchandising,* May 1987.

11. David Pinto, "What Constitutes a Food/Drug Combo?" *Mass Market Retailers,* 19 December 1988.

12. "Merchandising Condoms: Profits within Reach," *Convenience Store Merchandiser,* November 1987.

13. "Annual Report of the Chain Drug Industry."

14. John Kenneth Galbraith, *American Capitalism: The Theory of Countervailing Power* (Boston: Houghton Mifflin, 1952).

15. William G. Shepherd, *The Economics of Industrial Organization* (Englewood Cliffs, N.J.: Prentice-Hall, 1985), 287–88.

16. Oscar T. Bookings, "Concentrated Oligopsony with Leadership: Comment," *American Economist* 14, no. 2 (Fall 1970): 78.

17. Richard E. Just and Wen S. Chern, "Tomatoes, Technology, and Oligopsony," *Bell Journal of Economics* 11 (Autumn 1980): 584–602.

18. Steven H. Lustgarten, "The Impact of Buyer Concentration in Manufacturing Industries," *Review of Economics and Statistics* (May 1975): 125–32.

19. Steven H. Lustgarten, "The Use of Buyer Concentration Ratios in Tests of Oligopoly Models: Reply," *Review of Economics and Statistics* 58, no. 4 (November 1976): 492–94.

20. James McIntosh, "An Oligopolistic Model of Wage Determination in Agrarian Societies," *Economic Journal* 94 (September 1984): 569–79.

21. Lois A. Guth, Robert A. Schwartz, and David K. Whitcomb, "The Use of Buyer Concentration Ratios in Tests of Oligopoly Models," *Review of Economics and Statistics* (November 1976): 488–92.

22. Lois A. Guth, Robert A. Schwartz, and David K. Whitcomb, "Buyer Concentration Ratios," *Review of Economics and Statistics* 25 (June 1977): 241–58.

Chapter 5

1. *Contraceptive Technology Update,* November 1987.

2. J.B. Mason, M.L. Mayer, and H.F. Ezell, *Retailing* (Plano, Texas: Business Publications, 1988), chapter 14.

3. W.R. Davidson, D.J. Sweeney, and R.W. Stampfl, *Retailing Management* (New York: John Wiley & Sons, 1984), 314.

4. Philip H. Dougherty, "Condom Business Is Dropped," *New York Times,* 25 February 1987.

5. Colin Leinster, "The Rubber Barons," *Fortune,* 24 November 1986.

6. Seth Mendelson and Rob Lindstrom, "The Slotting Machine," *Non-Food Merchandising,* May 1987.

7. George Stigler, "The Literature of Economics: The Case of the Kinked Demand Curve," *Economic Inquiry* (April 1978): 185–204.

8. Davidson et al., *Retailing Management,* illustrates the interrelationships on p. 285 and the interaction of price and costs on p. 114.

9. Paul Sweezy, "Demand Under Conditions of Oligopoly," *Journal of Political Economy* 47 (1939): 568–73.

10. R.L. Hall and C.J. Hitch, "Price Theory and Economic Behavior," *Oxford Economic Papers* (1939), as described in Paolo Sylos-Labini, *Oligopoly and Technical Progress.*

11. Paolo Sylos-Labini, *Oligopoly and Technical Progress* (Cambridge: Harvard University Press, 1969), 25.

12. Ibid., 33–50.

13. Ibid., 50.

14. Willi Semmler, *Competition, Monopoly, and Differential Profit Rates* (New York: Columbia University Press, 1984).

15. Alfred Kahn, "Market Power Inflation: A Conceptual Overview," in John Blair, *The Roots of Inflation,* 255.

16. James Clifton, "Competition and the Evolution of the Capitalist Mode of Production," *Cambridge Journal of Economics* 1 (1977): 137–51.

17. Edward J. Nell, "Steady Prices in an Unsteady World," unpublished, 1989.

18. George Stigler, "The Kinky Oligopoly Demand Curve and Rigid Prices," *Journal of Political Economy* 55 (October 1947): 432–49.

19. William Baumol, "The Empirical Determination of Demand Relationships," in *Microeconomics: Selected Readings,* ed. Edwin Mansfield (New York: W.W. Norton & Co., 1979), 55.

20. Sylos-Labini, in *Oligopoly and Technical Progress,* wrote "A demand curve is imaginable in the abstract (but not practical)" (93). I assume he means not practical to quantify. The abstraction certainly has value in aiding our understanding.

21. Sylos-Labini, *Oligopoly and Technical Progress,* 52.

22. Technical change is limited in the condom industry. There is little opportunity to dramatically change the latex formulation in a way which will yield a competitive advantage. New condom designs, such as the self-adhering sheath developed by Mentor Corp. have not led to a sales revolution. Condom users are conservative. However, the possibility that a new product could capture a significant share (even if only within a specialized niche) remains.

23. G. Stigler, "The Literature of Economics," 192.

24. Sylos-Labini, *Oligopoly and Technical Progress,* 39, 53, 54.

25. Paul Sweezy, "Demand Under Conditions of Oligopoly," *Journal of Political Economy* 47 (1939): 568–73.

26. Semmler, in *Competition, Monopoly, and Differential Profit Rates,* reported that Demsetz found that "a persistence of profit rates among industries . . . results not from market power as measured by concentration but . . . from higher productivity of firms in concentrated industries."

Chapter 6

1. *Medical Device Amendments of 1976. Report by the House Committee on Interstate and Foreign Commerce* (Washington, D.C.: U.S. Government Printing Office, 1976).

2. *Medical Device Amendments,* 26.

3. *Code of Federal Regulations: Food and Drugs 21 Parts 800 to 1299 Revised as of April 1, 1987* (Washington, D.C.: Office of the Federal Register, National Archives and Record Administration, 1987).

4. *Good Manufacturing Practices for Medical Devices* (U.S. Department of Health, Education and Welfare, 1, Silver Springs, Md.: November 1979).

5. *Food and Drug Administration Compliance Policy Guides: Guide 7124.21,* chapter 24, "Devices," 10 April 1987.

6. Richard M. Cooper, "Clinical Data Under Section 510(k)," *Food, Drug, Cosmetics Law Journal* 42 (1987): 192–202.

7. April 7, 1987, letter from the FDA to U.S. condom manufacturers, importers, and repackagers.

8. Walter Adams, *The Structure of American Industry* (New York: Macmillan, 1986).

9. Ibid.

10. David Schwartzman, *Innovation in the Pharmaceutical Industry* (Baltimore: Johns Hopkins University Press, 1976), 300.

11. Joseph Jadlon, "A Summary and Critique of Economic Studies in the Ethical Drug Industry: 1962–1968," in *Issues in Pharmaceutical Economics*, ed. Robert I. Chien (Lexington, Mass.: Lexington Books/D.C. Heath Co., 1979), 13.

12. John R. Virts, "Economic Regulation of Prescription Drugs," *Issues in Pharmaceutical Economics*, 195.

13. Peter Barton Hutt, "A History of Government Regulation of Adulteration and Misbranding of Medical Devices," *Food and Drug Law Journal* 44, no. 2 (March 1989).

14. Rob S. McCutcheon, "Toxicology and the Law," in *Toxicology*, ed. Louis J. Casarett and John Doull (New York: Macmillan, 1975), 730.

15. Winifred Sewell, *Guide to Drug Information* (Hamilton, Ill.: Drug Intelligence Publications, 1976), cited similar procedures giving legal status to existing standards at the very start of the FDA in 1906 (25).

16. *Food and Drug Administration Policy Guide 7124.21*, dated 10 April 1987.

17. Center for Devices and Radiological Health, *Medical Devices Bulletin* 5, no. 5 (May 1987).

18. Schwartzman, *Innovation in the Pharmaceutical Industry*, 324.

19. Oswald H. Brownlee, "The Economic Consequences of Regulating without Regard to Economic Consequences," in *Issues in Pharmaceutical Economics*, 215.

Chapter 7

1. *Update on Condoms: Products, Protection, Promotion.* Population Reports Series H, no. 6, September–October 1982 (Baltimore: Johns Hopkins University Press).

2. William G. Shepherd, *The Economics of Industrial Organization* (Englewood Cliffs, N.J.: Prentice-Hall, 1985), 11.

3. U.S. Department of Health and Human Services, *Contraceptive Use in the United States, 1982.* DHHS Publication Number (PHS) 86–1988 (Hyattsville, Md., September 1986) J.D. Forrest and R.R. Fordyce, "U.S. Women's Contraceptive Attitudes and Practice: How Have They Changed in the 1980s?," *Family Planning Perspectives* (May–June 1988).

4. Gregory Spencer, *Projections of the Population of the United States by Age, Sex, and Race 1983 to 2080*, Series P-25 No. 292 (Washington, D.C.: U.S. Department of Health and Human Services, Bureau of the Census, May 1984).

5. *Advance Report of the Final Natality Statistics, 1984,* Monthly Vital Statistics Report 35, no. 4, Supplement (Washington, D.C., 18 July 1986).

6. Gregory Spencer, *Projections of the Population.*

7. Forrest and Fordyce, "U.S. Women's Contraceptive Attitudes and Practice."

8. *Update on Condoms.*

9. Asher Wolinsky, "True Monopolistic Competition as a Result of Imperfect Information," *Quarterly Journal of Economics* (August 1986): 493–511.

10. Shepherd, *Economics of Industrial Organization*, 215–16, 239–40.

11. William L. Sammon, Mark A. Kurland, and Robert Spitalnick, *Business Competitor Intelligence* (New York: John Wiley & Sons, 1984).

12. "More Unmarried Women Having Sex Despite AIDS Threat: Their Condom Use Increasing But Limited," Allan Guttmacher Institute *NEWS*, 28 July 1988.

13. Janet Lever, "Condoms and Collegians," *Playboy,* September 1988.

14. Centers for Disease Control, *AIDS Weekly Bulletin,* 11 April 1988, 6.

15. H.W. Haverkos, M.D., and R. Edelman, M.D., "The Epidemiology of Acquired Immunodeficiency Syndrome among Heterosexuals," *JAMA* (7 October 1988).

16. Forrest and Fordyce, "U.S. Women's Contraceptive Attitudes and Practice."

17. R.H. Bruskin Associates, *Study on Condom Awareness and Usage,* October 1987 (a private study completed for Schmid Laboratories).

18. *Update on Condoms.*

19. J.L. Martin, "The Impact of AIDS on Gay Male Sexual Behavior Patterns in New York City," *American Journal of Public Health* 77 (1987): 570–81.

20. *Designing an Effective AIDS Prevention Campaign Strategy for San Francisco* (San Francisco: Research and Design Corporation, Communications Technologies, 1986).

21. Lode Wigersma, M.D., "Safety and Acceptability of Condoms for Use by Homosexual Men as a Prophylactic Against Transmission of HIV During Anogenital Sexual Intercourse," *British Medical Journal* 295 (11 July 1987).

22. Franklyn Judson and J. Douglas, *Sexual Behavior and Knowledge of AIDS in Gay Men Diagnosed with Gonorrhea or Syphilis* (Paper presented at the Fourth International Conference on AIDS, Stockholm, Sweden, 12–16 June 1988).

23. N. Judson, *Fear of AIDS and Incidences of Gonorrhea, Syphilis, and Hepititis B, 1982–87* (Paper presented at the Fourth International Conference on AIDS, Stockholm, Sweden, 12–16 June 1988).

24. Christa Hookas et al., *Risk Perception of HIV Infection and Other STDs Among Heterosexuals with Many Sexual Partners* (Paper presented at the Fourth International Conference on AIDS, Stockholm, Sweden, 12–16 June 1988).

Chapter 8

1. William Pratt et al., Understanding U.S. Fertility: Findings from the National Survey of Family Growth, Cycle III, *Population Reference Bureau,* 39, no. 5 (December 1984).

2. D. Callahan, *11 Million Teenagers. What can be done about the Epidemic of Teenage Pregnancies in the United States?* (New York: Allen Guttmacher Institute, 1976).

3. National Center for Health Statistics, "Advance Report of Final Natality Statistics 1984," *Monthly Vital Statistics Report* 35, no. 4, Supplement (1986), Table 2.

4. M. Burt, "Estimating the Public Cost of Teenage Childbearing," *Family Planning Perspectives* 18, no. 5 (September–October 1986).

5. J.D. Forrest, "The United States," in *Teenage Pregnancy in Industrialized Countries,* ed. E.F. Jones et al. (New Haven: Yale University Press, 1986).

6. B. Kantrowitz et al., "Kids and Contraceptives," *Newsweek,* 16 February 1987.

7. M. Chamie and S.K. Henshaw, "The Costs and Benefits of Government Expenditures for Family Planning Programs," *Family Planning Perspectives* 13, no. 3 (May–June 1981).

8. S.J. Emans et al., "Adolescents' Compliance with the Use of Oral Contraceptives," *JAMA* (26 June 1987).

9. A.A. Scitovsky and D.P. Rice, "Estimates of the Direct and Indirect Costs

of Acquired Immunodeficiency Syndrome in the United States, 1985, 1986, 1991," *Public Health Reports* (January–February 1987).

10. Kantowitz et al., "Kids and Contraceptives."

11. J.W. Curran, M.D., "Economic Consequences of Pelvic Inflammatory Disease in the United States," *American Journal of Obstetrics/Gynecology* (1 December 1980).

12. A.E. Washington, M.D., et al., "The Economic Cost of Pelvic Inflammatory Disease," *JAMA* (4 April 1988).

13. Willard Cates, Jr., "The Other STDs: Do They Really Matter?" *JAMA* (24 June 1988): 3606–8.

14. Willard Cates, Jr., "How Justifiable Is Public Support of Sexually Transmitted Disease Clinical Services," *JAMA* (4 April 1986): 1769.

15. Ronald H. Coase, "The Problem of Social Cost," *Microeconomics: Selected Readings*, ed. Edwin Mansfield (New York: W.W. Norton & Co., 1979).

Chapter 9

1. William G. Shepherd, *The Economics of Industrial Organization* (Englewood Cliffs, N.J.: Prentice-Hall, 1985), 61.

2. H. Michael Mann, "Seller Concentration, Barriers to Entry, and Rates of Return in Thirty Industries: 1950–1960," *Review of Economics and Statistics* (August 1966): 296–307.

3. J.S. Bain, "Relation of Profit Rate to Industry Concentration: American Manufacturing 1936–40," *Quarterly Journal of Economics* (August 1951): 293–324.

4. David Qualls, "Barriers to Entry and Profit Margins," *Journal of Industrial Economics* 20, no. 2 (1972): 231–43.

5. Willi Semmler, *Competition, Monopoly, and Differential Profit Rates* (New York: Columbia University Press, 1984).

6. This point is discussed in Richard Schmalensee, "Economies of Scale and Barriers to Entry," *Journal of Political Economy* (December 1981): 1228–38.

7. C.C. von Weisaker, "A Welfare Analysis of Barriers to Entry," *Bell Journal of Economics* (Autumn 1980): 399.

8. Paul L. Jaskow, "Firm Decision-Making Processes and Oligopoly Theory," *American Economic Review* (May 1975): 278.

9. Irving Fisher, *Theory of Interest* (New York: Augustus M. Kelley, 1930).

10. J.M. Keynes, *The General Theory of Employment, Interest, and Money* (New York: Harcourt, Brace & World, 1935).

11. Pearson Hunt, Charles Williams and Gordon Donaldson, *Basic Business Finance* (Homewood, Ill.: Richard D. Irwin, 1958), 494–95.

12. Neil A. Doherty, *Corporate Risk Management* (New York: McGraw-Hill, 1985).

13. Ruth I. Kurtz, *Handbook of Engineering Economics* (New York: McGraw-Hill, 1984).

14. James C. Van Horne, *Financial Management and Policy* (Englewood Cliffs, N.J.: Prentice-Hall, 1986).

15. Fred Weston and Thomas E. Copeland, *Managerial Finance* (Chicago: Dryden Press, 1986).

16. Van Horne, *Financial Management*, 150.

17. Keynes, *General Theory*.

18. Robert Hayes and Ramchrandran Jaikumar, "Manufacturing's Crisis: New Technologies, Obsolete Organizations," *Harvard Business Review* (September–October, 1988).

19. Keynes, *General Theory*, 150.
20. Ibid., 154.
21. Ibid., 150.
22. Michael E. Porter, *Competitive Advantage* (New York: Free Press, 1985), 5.
23. Ibid., 6.
24. Ibid., 8.
25. Ibid., 9.
26. Ibid., 11.
27. The "value chain" is an application of the general approach known as systems analysis which has been in use at least since the 1960s. Bernard C. Reimann discusses this in his article "Sustaining the Competitive Advantage," *Planning Review* (March–April 1989): 30–39.

Bibliography

Books

Adams, Walter. *The Structure of American Industry.* New York: Macmillan, 1986.

Bain, Joe S. *Industrial Organization.* New York: John Wiley & Sons, 1968.

Beatie, Bruce R., and C. Robert Taylor. *The Economics of Production.* New York: John Wiley & Sons, 1985.

Blair, John Malcom. *Economic Concentration: Structure, Behavior, and Policy.* New York: Harcourt Brace Jovanovich, 1972.

Breedlove, E.B., et al. *Contraceptive Technology 1988–1989.* Atlanta: Printed Matter, 1988.

Callahan, D. *Eleven Million Teenagers: What Can Be Done About the Epidemic of Teenage Pregnancies in the United States?* New York: Allen Guttmacher Institute, 1976.

Casarett, Louis J., and John Doull, eds. *Toxicology.* New York: Macmillan, 1975.

Casanova, J. *Memoires de Jacques Casanova de Seingalt.* Brussels: J. Rosez, 1872.

Chien, Robert I., ed. *Issues in Pharmaceutical Economics.* Lexington, Mass: Lexington Books/D.C. Heath Co., 1979.

Davidson, W.R., D.J. Sweeney, and R.W. Stampfl. *Retailing Management.* New York: John Wiley & Sons, 1984.

Doherty, Neil A. *Corporate Risk Management.* New York: McGraw-Hill, 1985.

Dubeck, J. and M. Drozen. *Medical Devices and the Law.* Vienna, Va.: Cambridge Institute, 1988.

Edwards, Charles, ed. *The Competitive Status of the U.S. Pharmaceutical Industry.* Washington, D.C.: National Academy Press, 1976.

Ferguson, C.E. *Microeconomic Theory.* Homewood, Ill.: Richard D. Irwin, 1969.

Fisher, Irving. *Theory of Interest.* New York: Augustus M. Kelley, 1930.

Galbraith, John K. *American Capitalism: The Theory of Countervailing Power.* Boston: Houghton Mifflin, 1952.

Himes, Norman E. *Medical History of Contraception.* New York: Gamut Press, 1963.

Hunt, Pearson, Charles Williams, and Gordon Donaldson. *Basic Business Finance.* Homewood, Ill.: Richard D. Irwin, 1958.

Jones, E.F., et al. *Teenage Pregnancy in Industrialized Countries.* New Haven: Yale University Press, 1986.

Keynes, J.M. *The General Theory of Employment, Interest, and Money.* New York: Harcourt Brace & World, 1964.

Kurtz, Ruth I. *Handbook of Engineering Economics.* New York: McGraw-Hill, 1984.

Mansfield, Edwin, ed. *Microeconomics: Selected Readings.* New York: W.W. Norton & Co., 1979.

Mason, J.B., R.L. Mayer, and H.P. Ezell. *Retailing.* Plano, Texas: Business Publications, 1988.

Matoren, Gary M., ed. *The Clinical Research Process in the Pharmaceutical Industry.* New York: Marcel Dekker, 1984.

Mausser, R.F. *The Vanderbilt Latex Handbook.* Norwalk, Conn.: R.T. Vanderbilt, 1987.

Merkin, Donald H. *Pregnancy as a Disease.* Port Washington, N.Y.: Kennikat Press, 1976.

National Academy of Sciences. *Rapid Population Growth: Consequences and Policy Implications.* Baltimore: Johns Hopkins University Press, 1971.

Nortman, D.L. et al. *Birth Rates and Birth Control Practice.* New York: Population Council, 1978.

Pigou, A.C. *Economics of Welfare.* London: Macmillan, 1952.

Porter, Michael E. *Competitive Advantage.* New York: Free Press, 1985.

Rainwater, Lee. *Family Design: Marital Sexuality, Family Size, and Contraception.* Chicago: Aldine, 1965.

Redford, Duncan, and Prager Redford. *The Condom: Increasing Utilization in the United States.* San Francisco: San Francisco Press, 1974.

Rinear, Charles E. *The Sexually Transmitted Diseases.* Jefferson, N.C.: McFarland & Co., 1986.

Robinson, Joan. *What Are the Questions? and Other Essays.* Armonk, N.Y.: M.E. Sharpe, 1980.

Sammon, William L., Mark A. Kurland, and Robert Spitalnick. *Business Competitor Intelligence.* New York: John Wiley & Sons, 1984.

San Francisco Research and Design Corporation. *Designing and Effective AIDS Prevention Campaign Strategy for San Francisco.* San Francisco: Communications Technologies, 1986.

Sanger, Margaret. *Women and the New Race.* New York: Brentano's, 1920.

Schwartzman, David. *Innovation in the Pharmaceutical Industry.* Baltimore: Johns Hopkins University Press, 1976.

Semmler, Willi. *Competition, Monopoly, and Differential Profit Rates.* New York: Columbia University Press, 1984.

Sewell, Winifred. *Guide to Drug Information.* Hamilton, Ill.: Drug Intelligence Publications, 1976.

Shapiro, Howard L. *The Birth Control Book.* New York: St. Martin's Press, 1988.

Shepherd, William G. *The Economics of Industrial Organization.* Englewood Cliffs, N.J.: Prentice-Hall, 1985.

Spencer, G. *Projections of the Population of the United States by Age, Sex, and Race 1983 to 2080.* Washington, D.C.: U.S. Bureau of the Census, 1984.

Stigler, G.J. *The Theory of Price.* New York: Macmillan, 1952.

Stonier, A.W., and D.C. Hague. *A Textbook of Economic Theory.* London: Longmans, Green and Co., 1953.

Sylos-Labini, Paolo. *Oligopoly and Technical Progress.* Cambridge: Harvard University Press, 1969.

U.S. Congress. House of Representatives. Committee on Interstate and Foreign Commerce. *Medical Device Amendments of 1976.* Washington, D.C.: U.S. Government Printing Office, 1976.

U.S. Department of Health and Human Services. *Contraceptive Use in the United States,* 1982 DHHS Publication No. (PHS)86–1988. Washington, D.C.: U.S. Government Printing Office, 1986.

U.S. Department of Health, Education and Welfare. *Good Manufacturing Practices for Medical Devices.* Washington, D.C.: U.S. Government Printing Office, 1979.

U.S. Food and Drug Administration. *Food and Drug Administration Compliance*

Policy Guides. Guide 7124.12. Washington, D.C.: U.S. Government Printing Office, 1987.

Van Horne, James C. *Financial Management and Policy.* Englewood Cliffs, N.J.: Prentice-Hall, 1986.

Washington Office of the Federal Register, National Archives and Record Administration. *Code of Federal Regulations. Food and Drugs 21 Parts 800 to 1299 Revised as of April 1, 1987.* Washington, D.C.: U.S. Government Printing Office, 1987.

Weiss, Leonard W. *Case Studies in American Industry.* New York: John Wiley & Sons, 1967.

Weston, J. Fred, and Thomas E. Copeland. *Managerial Finance.* Chicago: Dryden Press, 1986.

Winspear, G., ed. *The Vanderbilt Rubber Handbook.* New York: R.T. Vanderbilt Co., 1958.

Articles

"Advance Report of the Final Natality Statistics, 1984." *Monthly Vital Statistics Report* 34, no. 4, Supplement (18 July 1986).

Atmore, M. "NFM's Exclusive Report on Space Allotment, Turns, and Promotion Paints a Picture at Retail." *Non-Food Merchandising* (May 1987).

Bain, J.S. "Relation of Profit Rate to Industry Concentration: American Manufacturing 1936–40." *Quarterly Journal of Economics* (August 1951): 1024–48.

Bookings, Oscar T. "Concentrated Oligopsony with Leadership: Comment." *American Economist* 14 (Fall 1970): 78.

Burt, M. "Estimating the Public Cost of Teenage Childbearing." *Family Planning Perspectives* 18, no. 5 (September–October 1986).

Buxton, Anthony J. "The Kinked Demand Model and Limit Pricing." *Bulletin of Economic Research* (November 1982): 115–23.

Casey, William L., Jr., and Surendra Kaushik. "The Kinked-Demand Model of Oligopoly: Textbook Departures from the Original Sweezy Model." *American Economist* (Fall 1982): 25–32. **Also see:** "The Improper Derivation of Marginal Revenue in Kinky Oligopoly Models: A Reply to 'The Kinked-Demand Model of Oligopoly: Textbook Departures from the Original Sweezy Model.'" *American Economist* (Fall 1984): 89. **Also see:** Lombardy [below].

Cates, Willard, Jr. "How Justifiable Is Public Support of Sexually Transmitted Disease Clinical Services?" *JAMA* (4 April 1986).

________. "The Other STDs: Do They Really Matter? *JAMA* (24 June 1986): 3606–8.

"Chains vs. Independents: A Decade of Change." *Drug Store News,* 13 April 1987.

Chang, Chen Fu. "The Firm's Long-Run Average Cost Curve." *Quarterly Review of Economics and Business* (Winter 1969).

Chamie, M., and S. Henshaw. "The Costs and Benefits of Government Expenditures for Family Planning Programs." *Family Planning Perspectives* 13, no. 3 (May–June 1981).

Clifton, James A. "Competition and the Evolution of the Capitalist Mode of Production." *Cambridge Journal of Economics* 1 (1977): 137–51.

Cooper, R.M. "Clinical Data under Section 510(k)." *Food, Drug, Cosmetics Law Journal* 42 (1987): 192–202.

Cowley, P.R. "Business Margins and Buyer/Seller Power." *Review of Economics and Statistics* (May 1986): 333–37.

Curran, J.W. "Economic Consequences of Pelvic Inflammatory Diseases in the

United States." *American Journal of Obstetrics/Gynecology* (December 1980).

Demsetz, Harold. "Barriers to Entry." *American Economic Review* (March 1982): 47–57.

Emans, S., et al. "Adolescents' Compliance with the Use of Oral Contraceptives." *JAMA* (26 June 1987).

Forrest, J.D. and R.R. Fordyce. "U.S. Women's Contraceptive Attitudes and Practice: How Have They Changed in the 1980s? *Family Planning Perspectives* (May–June 1988).

Goldberg, Howard J. "Worldwide Use of Condoms." Paper presented at the *Conference on Condoms in the Prevention of Sexually Transmitted Diseases* held in Atlanta, Ga., 20 February 1987.

Guth, Lois A., Robert A. Swartz, and David K. Whitcomb. "The Use of Buyer Concentration Ratios in Tests of Oligopoly Models." *Review of Economics and Statistics* (November 1976): 488–92.

________. "Buyer Concentration Ratios." *Review of Economics and Statistics* 25 (June 1977): 241–58.

Hall, Robert L., and C.J. Hitch. "Price Theory and Economic Behavior." *Oxford Economic Papers* (1939).

Hanoch, Giora. "The Elasticity of Scale and the Shape of Average Cost Curves." *American Economic Review* (June 1975): 492–97.

Haverkos, H., and R. Edelman. "The Epidemiology of Acquired Immunodeficency Syndrome Among Heterosexuals." *JAMA* (7 October 1988).

Hayes, Robert H., and Ramchrandran Jaikumar. "Manufacturing's Crisis; New Technologies, Obsolete Organizations." *Harvard Business Review* (September–October 1988).

Hookas, C., et al. "Risk Perception of HIV Infection and Other STDs Among Heterosexuals with Many Sexual Partners." Paper delivered at the Fourth International Conference on AIDS, Stockholm, Sweden, 12–16 June 1988.

Hutt, Peter Barton. "A History of Government Regulation of Adulteration and Misbranding of Medical Devices." *Food and Drug Law Journal* 44, no. 2 (March 1989).

Joskow, Paul L. "Firm Decision-Making Processes and Oligopoly Theory." *American Economic Review* (May 1975): 270–83.

Judson, N. "Fear of AIDS and Incidences of Gonorrhea, Syphilis, and Hepatitis B, 1982–87." Paper delivered at the Fourth Conference on AIDS, Stockholm, Sweden, 12–16 June 1988.

________. "Sexual Behavior and Knowledge of AIDS in Gay Men Diagnosed with Gonorrhea and Syphilis." Paper delivered at the Fourth International Conference on AIDS, Stockholm, Sweden, 12–16 June 1988

Just, Richard E., and Wen S. Chern. "Tomatoes, Technology, and Oligopsony." *Bell Journal of Economics* (Autumn 1980): 584–602.

Kelly, William A., and Donald M. Waldman. "A Generalized Economic/Uneconomic Boundary for Short-Run Product and Cost Curves." *Atlantic Economic Journal* 4 (December 1982): 82–85.

Kessler, D.A., et al. "The Federal Regulation of Medical Devices." *New England Journal of Medicine* (6 August 1987).

LaFrance, V.A. "Impact of Buyer Concentration—An Extension." *Review of Economics and Statistics* (August 1979): 475–76.

Leinster, Colin. "The Rubber Barons." *Fortune,* 24 November 1986.

Lever, J. "Condoms and Collegians." *Playboy,* September 1988.

Lombardy, Waldo John. "A Note on 'The Improper Derivation of Marginal Revenue in Kinky Oligopoly Models: A Reply to "The Kinked-Demand Model of

Oligopoly: Textbook Departures from the Original Sweezy Model.''' *American Economist* (Fall 1984): 87–88.

Lustgarten, Steven H. "The Impact of Buyer Concentration in Manufacturing Industries." *Review of Economics and Statistics* (May 1975): 125–32.

———. "The Use of Buyer Concentration Ratios in Tests of Oligopoly Models: Reply." *Review of Economics and Statistics* 58, no. 4 (November 1976): 492–94.

McIntosh, James. "An Oligopolistic Model of Wage Determination in Agrarian Societies." *Economic Journal* (September 1984): 569–79.

Mann, H. Michael. "Seller Concentration, Barriers to Entry, and Rates of Return in Thirty Industries, 1950–1960." *Review of Economics and Statistics* 48 (August 1966): 296–307.

Martin, J.L. "The Impact of AIDS on Gay Male Sexual Behavior Patterns in New York City." *American Journal of Public Health* 77 (1987): 578–81.

Mendelson, Seth, and Rob Lindstrom. "The Slotting Machine." *Non-Food Merchandising,* May 1987.

"Merchandising Condoms: Profits within Reach." *Convenience Store Merchandiser,* November 1987.

"More Unmarried Women Having Sex Despite AIDS Threat: The Condom Use Increasing but Limited." *NEWS,* 28 July 1988.

Pechter, K. "Gentlemen Prefer Condoms." *Men's Health,* Spring 1986.

Pfouts, R.W. "Profit Maximization in Chain Retail Stores." *Journal of Industrial Economics* (September 1970): 69–83.

Pinto, D. "What Constitutes a Food/Drug Combo?" *Mass Market Retailers,* 19 December 1988.

Pratt, W. "Understanding U.S. Fertility: Findings from the National Survey of Family Growth, Cycle III." *Population Reference Bureau Inc.* 39, no. 5 (December 1984).

Primeaux, Walter J., and Mark R. Bomall. "A Reexamination of the Kinky Oligopoly Demand Curve." *Journal of Political Economy* (July–August 1974): 851–62.

Qualls, David. "Concentration, Barriers to Entry, and Long-Run Economic Profit Margins." *Journal of Industrial Economics* 20, no. 2 (1972): 231–42.

Reiman, Bernard C. "Sustaining the Competitive Advantage." *Planning Review* (March–April 1989): 30–39.

Revier, Charles. "The Elasticity of Scale, the Shape of Average Costs, and the Envelope Theorem." *American Economic Review* (June 1987).

Roosevelt, Theodore. "Race Decadence." *Outlook,* 8 April 1911.

Rowe, John M. "Short-Run, Long-Run, and Vector Cost Curves." *Southern Economic Journal* (January 1971): 245–50.

Schmalensee, Richard. "Economies of Scale and Barriers to Entry." *Journal of Political Economy* (December 1981): 1228–38.

Schraffler, R. "Fuji Plans 2nd U.S. Condom Plant." *Rubber and Plastic News,* January 1988.

Scitovsky, A.A., and D.P. Rice. "Estimates of the Direct and Indirect Costs of Acquired Immunodeficiency Syndrome in the United States, 1985, 1986, 1991." *Public Health Reports* (January–February 1987).

Shaanan, Joseph. "Welfare and Barriers to Entry: An Empirical Study." *Southern Economic Journal* (January 1988): 746–62.

Shepherd, A. Ross. "Notes: The Firm's Long-Run Cost Curve." *Quarterly Review of Economics and Business* (Spring 1971).

Shuster, Bierman, and Perlman. "The ABCs of Condoms." *Private Label,* November–December 1987.

Simon, Julian. "A Further Test of the Kinky Oligopoly Demand Curve." *American Economic Review* (December 1969): 971–75.

Spulber, Daniel F. "Scale Economies and Sustainable Monopoly Prices." *Journal of Economic Theory* (October 1984): 149–49.

Stigler, George. "The Kinky Oligopoly Demand Curve and Rigid Prices." *Journal of Political Economy* 55 (October 1947): 432–49.

________. "The Literature of Economics: The Case of the Kinked Demand Curve." *Economic Inquiry* (April 1978): 185–204.

Stiglitz, Joseph E. "Competition and the Number of Firms in a Market: Are Duopolies More Competitive than Atomistic Markets?" *Journal of Political Economy* (October 1987): 1041–61.

Sweezy, Paul. "Demand Under Conditions of Oligopoly." *Journal of Political Economy* 47 (1939): 568–73.

Tatum, H., and E. Connel-Tatum. "Barrier Contraception: A Comprehensive Overview." *Fertility and Sterility* 36, no. 1 (July 1981).

"Update on Condoms—Products, Protection, Promotion." *Population Reports*, series H, no. 6 (September–October 1982).

Vanlommel, E., and B. DeBrabander. "Price-Cost Margins and Market Structure." *Journal of Industrial Economics* (September 1979): 1–22.

Washington, A.E., et al. "The Economic Cost of Pelvic Inflammatory Disease." *JAMA* (4 April 1982).

Whitten, David O. "A Flat-Kinked Demand Curve Function for Oligopolistic Sellers of Homogeneous Products." *Review of Industrial Organization* (Fall 1984): 206–15.

Wigersma, L. "Safety and Acceptability of Condoms for Use by Homosexual Men as a Prophylactic Against Transmission of HIV During Anogenital Sexual Intercourse." *British Medical Journal* 295 (11 July 1987).

Wolinsky, A. "True Monopolistic Competition as a Result of Imperfect Information." *Quarterly Journal of Economics* (August 1986): 493–511.

Company Reports

Ansell International. *Ansell.* Australia, 1987.

Carter-Wallace, Inc. *Annual Report for Year Ending March 31, 1988.*

London International Group. *Annual Report for Year Ending March 31, 1988.*

Schmid Laboratories. *One Hundred Years of Quality and Innovation in Personal Care Products: 1883–1983.*

Carter-Wallace. *The Age of the Condom.*

Interviews

Baker, Samuel. Retired vice-president for sales for Schmid Laboratories Inc. with over twenty-five years experience in the condom business.

Buza, Robert. Sales manager for Barnett, Inc., a leading supplier of condom vending machines and condoms.

Dougatch, Stanley. Executive vice-president for sales, National Sanitary Laboratories Inc., the largest supplier of condoms for vending machines.

Els, Larry. Director National Automatic Merchandising Association.

Frank, Philip. Retired director of medical marketing and member of the board of directors of the Youngs Rubber Company.

Goodhart, Fran. Director of health education, Rutgers University.

Horton, Peggy. Corporate secretary of PHE Inc., the leading supplier of condoms via mail orders.

Killian, Joseph "Jack." Son of Burchart S. Killian, inventor of the automated process for making condoms from natural rubber latex, president of Killian Latex, and a career-long executive in the rubber latex business.

Stanford, Tim. Editor, *Vending Times Magazine.*

Stone, David. Editor, *American Automatic Merchandiser.*

Index